# INTRODUCTION

The oceans and seas cover almost three-quarters of the surface of the Earth, and hidden in their depths are the largest animals on our planet. The blue whale is many times the size of an elephant, even bigger than the largest dinosaur —in fact, it is the largest animal ever known to have lived on Earth. Its living cousins are not much smaller—fin, sei, and Bryde's whales, not to mention humpbacks, grays, bowheads and right whales. These are all animals that are larger than every other living creature alive today, but they are not the only giants.

**MEGAMOUTH** was discovered as recently as 1976. Nobody knew this 16ft-long, deep-sea, filter feeder lived in the oceans until then.

The aptly named whale shark is the largest fish in the sea. It is the length of a school bus, dwarfing all but the giant baleen whale, and it shares with them their preference for feeding on the smallest creatures —tiny fish, krill and plankton. It lives in the tropics, but there are two other giants that are found elsewhere in the world. The basking shark skims the plankton-rich surface waters in temperate seas, and the newly discovered megamouth sieves the cold, twilight zone in mid-waters for deep-sea shrimps.

These amazing creatures are the gentle giants of the ocean realm, but there are also the hunters—the predators—and some of them are big, too. There are the largest and fastest of the whales—the killer whales. They are known as the "wolves of the sea" on account of their hunting in packs. A pack or pod can chase and wear down an animal the size of a blue whale, and then kill it, taking no more than its delicate tongue.

Representing the giant whales is the formidable sperm whale—Captain Ahab's adversary in Moby Dick—a toothed whale that plumbs the depths of the abyss in search of the biggest animal without a backbone—the giant squid. Nobody has witnessed the titanic battles down there, but plenty is known about other aspects of a sperm whale's life, and also about the lives of the other giants. This book is packed with the latest research on whale and shark biology. So, take an in-depth look at the way their bodies work and how they behave—how they feed, reproduce, interact with others of their own kind, and escape from creatures that might try to harm them.

**SPERM WHALE** The 60ft-long sperm whale is the largest toothed whale. It dives into the abyss to a depth of 6500ft in search of squid and deep-sea sharks.

# GIANTS OF THE OCEAN

Michael Bright and Robin Kerrod

Consultant
Ian K. Fergusson

southwater

This edition is published by Southwater

Southwater is an imprint of Anness Publishing Ltd
Hermes House, 88–89 Blackfriars Road, London SE1 8HA
tel. 020 7401 2077; fax 020 7633 9499
www.southwaterbooks.com; info@anness.com

UK agent: The Manning Partnership Ltd, 6 The Old Dairy,
Melcombe Road, Bath BA2 3LR
tel. 01225 478444; fax 01225 478440; sales@manning-partnership.co.uk

UK distributor: Grantham Book Services Ltd, Isaac Newton Way,
Alma Park Industrial Estate, Grantham, Lincs NG31 9SD
tel. 01476 541080; fax 01476 541061; orders@gbs.tbs-ltd.co.uk

North American agent/distributor: National Book Network,
4501 Forbes Boulevard, Suite 200, Lanham, MD 20706
tel. 301 459 3366; fax 301 429 5746; www.nbnbooks.com

Australian agent/distributor: Pan Macmillan Australia,
Level 18, St Martins Tower, 31 Market St, Sydney, NSW 2000
tel. 1300 135 113; fax 1300 135 103; customer.service@macmillan.com.au

New Zealand agent/distributor: David Bateman Ltd,
30 Tarndale Grove, Off Bush Road, Albany, Auckland
tel. (09) 415 7664; fax (09) 415 8892

A CIP catalogue record for this book is available from the British Library.

10 9 8 7 6 5 4 3 2 1

Publisher: Joanna Lorenz
Senior Editor: Sarah Uttridge
Editor: Elizabeth Woodland
Illustrators: Julian Baker, Stuart Carter, Vanessa Card
and David Webb
Jacket Design: Dean Price
DTP: Neil Mclaren
Production Controller: Darren Price

Previously published in two separate volumes,
*Nature Watch: Sharks* and *Nature Watch: Whales and Dolphins*

# CONTENTS

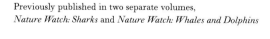

When it comes to harm, there is probably nothing scarier than the behavior of fish that trigger the worst of human fears—that of being eaten alive, and the creatures that do this are the predatory sharks. There are great white sharks and tiger sharks—numbers 1 and 2 in the shark attack league table—that search the surface waters, and there are sleeper sharks and six-gill sharks, both giants in their own right, that scour the darkness of the abyss. Sharks were once the stuff of nightmares—row upon row of razor-sharp teeth attached to powerful, flexible bodies that can slam into a target and take it out with one enormous bite. However, like whales, they are threatened. In fact, sharks are in more danger from people than people are from sharks. Over a million sharks are killed each year—harvested for their fins, jaws, liver oil or cartilage.

**BLUE WHALE**
The blue whale is the largest baleen whale with a maximum-recorded length of 100ft and an estimated weight in excess of 165 tons.

The attitude of many people towards sharks, however, is changing. Like whales and dolphins, sharks are being appreciated. Today, there is a campaign to hug rather than harm them. Gradually they are being seen as the remarkably sophisticated beasts that they really are, rather than the monsters they were once thought to be, and in this book you can read why.

**WHALE SHARK**
At 40ft long, the whale shark is the largest of the fishes. It is a filter feeder, like the baleen whales, and it is not dangerous unless you are hit accidentally by the large and powerful tail fin.

The problem is that we have failed to understand these animals and the way they work. Marine research is often an expensive undertaking, what with ships, submersibles and all the gear that goes with underwater exploration, so it has been severely limited. Yet, scientists have realized that the health of the sea and the creatures in it give us an early indication of when things are going wrong on our planet. Whales, dolphins and sharks are at the top of their food chains and therefore vulnerable to change. They are the ones that suffer when, say, pesticides enter the food chain and are concentrated at each link until they cause harm to the animals at the top. They are like the coal miners' canaries. So, there is a renaissance in marine biology as researchers look for the answers to today's environmental problems. The secrets of the world in which we live may be locked up in the remarkable creatures that we call the "giants of the ocean".

**GREAT WHITE SHARK**

The great white shark is reputed to reach a length of 36ft, but specimens today rarely exceed 20ft.

# WHALES

Whales must visit the sea's surface regularly in order to breathe, or they will drown. They must also avoid "the bends" when they move into surface waters from the deep. To do this they must stop bubbles of gas from forming in their blood, so they collapse their lungs and "hide" the dissolved air in their muscles and other organs, where it can do no harm.

# Whale Order

Like fish, whales and dolphins spend all their lives in the sea. But unlike fish, they breathe air, have warm blood and suckle their young. They are more closely related to human beings than fish because they are mammals. Many whales are enormous—some are as big and as heavy as a train car full of passengers. Dolphins are much smaller—most are about the same size as an adult human being. Porpoises, which look much like dolphins, are also roughly the same size as humans. Although smaller, dolphins and porpoises are kinds of whales, too. All whales belong to the major group, or order, of animals called Cetacea.

## ▲ HEAVYWEIGHTS

The largest of the whales are the biggest animals ever to have lived. This leaping humpback whale is nearly 50 ft long and weighs over 25 tons—as much as five fully-grown elephants. Some other kinds of whales, such as the fin and blue whales, are much bigger.

## ▶ WHALE ANCESTORS

More than 50 million years ago, creatures like this were swimming in the seas. They seem to have been ancestors of modern cetaceans. This creature, named basilosaurus (meaning king lizard), grew up to over 65 ft long. It had a snake-like body with tiny front flippers and traces of a pair of hind limbs.

## ▼ BALEEN WHALES

These humpback whales are feeding in Alaskan waters. They belong to the group, or suborder, of whales known as the baleen whales. These are in general much larger than those in the other main group, the toothed whales.

### Whale in the Sky

*This star map shows a constellation of stars named Cetus, meaning the sea monster or whale. In Greek mythology, Cetus was a monster that was about to eat Andromeda, a maiden who had been chained to a rock as a sacrifice. Along came Perseus, who killed the sea monster and saved Andromeda.*

### ▲ TOOTHED WHALES

A bottlenose dolphin opens its mouth and shows its teeth. It is one of the many species of toothed whales. Toothed whales have much simpler teeth than land mammals and many more of them. The bottlenose dolphin, for example, has up to 50 teeth in both its upper and lower jaws.

### ◄ BREATHING

Because they are mammals, whales and dolphins breathe air. This common dolphin breathes out through a blowhole on top of its head as it rises to the surface. It can hold its breath for five minutes or more when diving.

*Did you know? A blue whale can weigh as much as 25 elephants.*

# Whales Large and Small

Most large whales belong to the major group of cetaceans called the baleen whales. Instead of teeth, these whales have brush-like plates, called baleen, that hang from their upper jaw. They use the baleen to filter food from the water. The sperm whale does not belong to the baleen group. It belongs to the other major cetacean group, called the toothed whales. This group also includes dolphins, porpoises, white whales and beaked whales.

▲ **GRAY WHALE**

The gray whale can grow up to nearly 50 ft long, and tip the scales at 35 tons or more. It is a similar size to the humpback, sei, bowhead and right whales, but looks quite different. Instead of the smooth skin of other whales, the gray has rough skin and no proper dorsal fin on its back.

*Did you know? Some whales have as many as 3,000 baleen plates in their jaws.*

▲ **BLACK AND WHITE**

The bowhead whale, which has a highly curved jaw, grows to 52 ft. It is closely related to the right whale. The bowhead is famous for its long baleen plates and thick layer of blubber. The toothed whales we call belugas *(above left)* grow to about 15 ft at most. The first part of the word beluga means white in Russian, and belugas are also known as white whales.

## ▶ SEI WHALE

At up to about 52 ft, the sei whale looks much like its bigger relatives, the blue whale and the fin. All are members of the group called rorquals, which have deep grooves in their throat. These grooves let the throat expand to take big mouthfuls of water for feeding. Seis have up to 60 grooves in their throat.

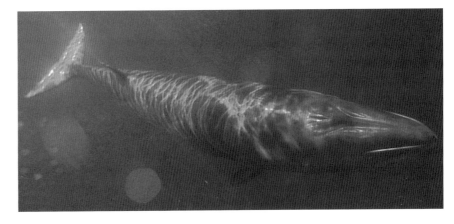

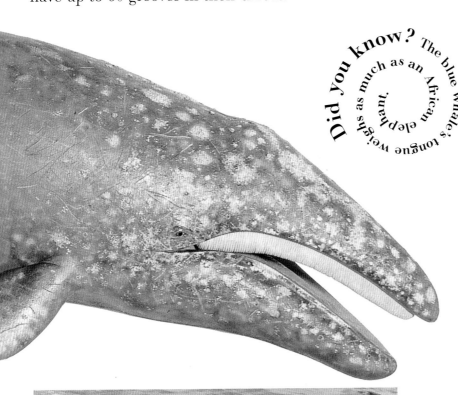

Did you know? The blue whale's tongue weighs as much as an African elephant.

## ▶ RELATIVE SIZES

Whales come in many sizes, from dolphins smaller than a human to the enormous blue whale, which can grow to 98 ft or more. In general, the baleen whales are much bigger than the toothed whales. The exception is the sperm whale, which can grow up to 62 ft.

porpoise

dolphin

narwhal

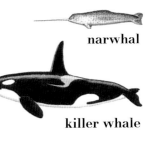
killer whale

beaked whale

gray whale

sperm whale

right whale

blue whale

## ▲ RISSO'S DOLPHIN

The dolphin pictured leaping here is a Risso's dolphin. It has a blunt snout and as few as six teeth. Most of the toothed whales that we call dolphins are on average between about 6 and 10 ft long. Risso's dolphins can grow a little bigger—up to nearly 13 ft long.

# Whale Bones

Like all mammals, whales have a skeleton of bones to give the body its shape and protect vital organs like the heart. Because a whale's body is supported by water, its bones are not as strong as those of land mammals, and are quite soft. The backbone is made up of many vertebrae, with joints in between to give it flexibility. While providing some body support, the backbone acts mainly as an anchor for the muscles, particularly the strong muscles that drive the tail. Instead of limbs, a whale has a pair of modified fore limbs, called flippers.

◄ **BONE CORSET**
This advertisement for a "whalebone" corset dates from 1911, a time when women wore corsets to give them shapely figures. The corsets were, in fact, made from the baleen plates found in whales' mouths.

▶ **UNDERNEATH THE ARCHES**
Arches built from the jaw bones of huge baleen whales can be seen in some ports that were once the home of whaling fleets. This jaw bone arch can be seen outside Christ Church Cathedral in Port Stanley, Falkland Islands. Nowadays, whales are protected species and building such arches is forbidden.

▶ **HANDS UP**
The bones in a sperm whale's flipper are remarkably similar to those in a human hand. A whale's flippers are a much changed version of a typical mammal's front limbs. Both hands have wrist bones, finger bones and joints.

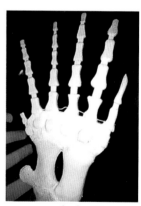

sperm whale flipper

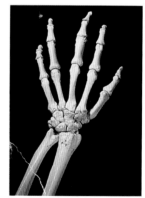

human hand

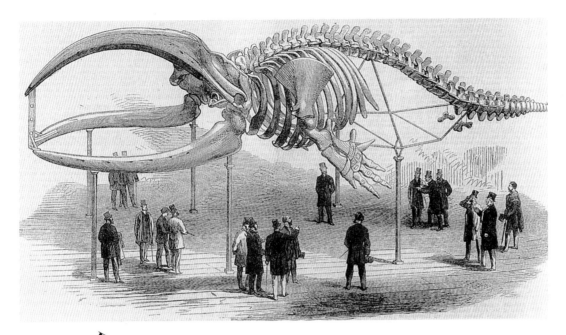

### ◄ BIG HEAD

This right whale skeleton was displayed in London in 1830. Its large jaw bones tell us that it is a baleen whale, which needs a big mouth for feeding. Like other mammals, it has a large rib cage to protect its body organs. However, it has no hind limbs or pelvic girdle.

Did you know? Whales are very oily and have a very strong smell.

### ▼ TOOTHY JAW

This is the skeleton of a false killer whale, one of the toothed whales. The head is much smaller than that of the baleen whales, and its jaws are studded with teeth. Its long spine is made up of segments called vertebrae. The vertebrae in the whale's waist region are large, so that they are strong enough to anchor the animal's powerful tail muscles.

### ▼ KILLER SKULL

Both jaws of this killer whale skull are studded with vicious, curved teeth that are more than 4 in. long. The killer whale is a deadly predator, attacking seals, dolphins and sometimes whales that are even bigger than itself.

# Whale Bodies

Over many millions of years, whales have developed features that suit them to a life spent mostly underwater. They have long, rounded bodies and smooth, almost hairless skin. Like fish, whales move around using fins. They have the same body organs, such as heart and lungs, as land mammals. In the big whales, however, the body organs are much larger than in land mammals.

## ▼ BIG MOUTH

This gray whale is one of the baleen whales, and the baleen can be seen hanging from its upper jaw. Baleen whales need a big mouth so that they can take in large mouthfuls of water when they are feeding. Gray whales usually feed at the bottom of the sea.

baleen

### Jonah and the Whale

*This picture from the 17th century tells one of the best known of all Bible stories. The prophet Jonah was thrown overboard by sailors during a terrible storm. To rescue him, God sent a whale, which swallowed him whole. Jonah spent three days in the whale's belly before it coughed him up onto dry land. The picture shows that many people at this time had little idea of what a whale looked like. The artist has given it shark-like teeth and a curly tail.*

## ▼ LEAPING DOLPHINS

A pair of bottlenose dolphins leaps effortlessly several yards out of the water. Powerful muscles near the tail provide them with the energy for fast swimming and leaping. They leap for various reasons—to signal to each other, to look for fish or perhaps just for fun.

## ▲ HANGERS ON

This humpback whale's throat is covered with barnacles, which take hold because the whale moves slowly. They cannot easily cling to swifter-moving cetaceans, such as dolphins. A dolphin sloughs off rough skin as it moves through the water. This also makes it harder for a barnacle to take hold.

## ▶ LOUSY WHALES

The gray whale's skin is covered with light-colored patches. These patches are clusters of ten-legged lice, called cyamids, about ¾ to 1¼ in. long. They feed on the whale's skin.

## ◀ BODY LINES

A pod, or group, of melon-headed whales swim in the Pacific Ocean. This species is one of the smaller whales, at less than 10 ft long. It shows the features of a typical cetacean—a well-rounded body with a short neck and a single fin. It has a pair of paddle-like front flippers and a tail with horizontal flukes.

Did you know? Whales have whiskers on their faces.

15

# Staying Alive

Whales are warm-blooded creatures. To stay alive, they must keep their bodies at a temperature of about 96.8-98.6°F. They swim in very cold water that quickly takes heat away from the surface of their bodies. To stop body heat from reaching the surface, whales have a thick layer of a fatty substance called blubber just beneath the skin. Whales must also breathe to stay alive. They breathe through a blowhole, situated on top of the head. When a whale breathes out, it sends a column of steamy water vapor high into the air.

epidermis

blood vessels

layer of blubber

**▲ IN THE WARM**
Southern right whales feed in icy Antarctic waters in summer. The whales' size helps limit the percentage of body heat they lose to the water.

**◄ SKIN DEEP**
This is a cross-section of a whale's outer layer. Beneath its skin, a thick layer of blubber insulates it from ice-cold water.

**► SMALL BODY**
Atlantic spotted dolphins are about the size of humans. Because it is small, its body has a relatively large surface area for its size and so loses heat faster than its big relatives. This is probably why the Atlantic spotted dolphin lives in warm waters.

Did you know? The body temperature of a whale is about the same as yours.

▶ SKY HIGH

A humpback whale surfaces and blows a column of warm, moist air. As it rises it cools, and the moisture in it condenses into a cloud of tiny water droplets.

▼ DEEP DIVING

Whales feed at different depths. Most dolphins feed close to the surface. The sperm whale holds the diving record, being able to descend to about 6,500 ft and stay under water for up to an hour.

| Depth | Length of Dive |
|---|---|
| Surface | common dolphin 15 minutes |
| | fin whale 20 minutes |
| 2000 ft | pilot whale 15 minutes |
| 4000 ft | |
| 6000 ft | |
| | sperm whale 60 minutes |
| 8000 ft | |

▼ ONE BLOWHOLE

Like all toothed whales, a bottlenose dolphin has only one blowhole. When the dolphin dives, thick lips of elastic tissue close it to stop water from entering, no matter how deep the dive.

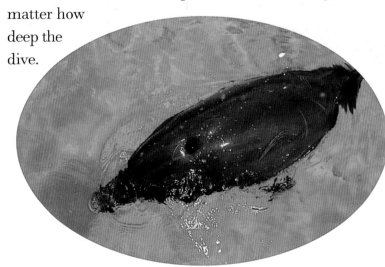

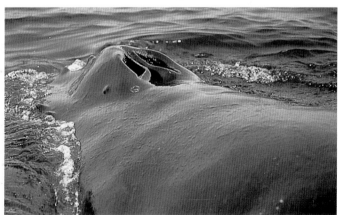

▲ TWO BLOWHOLES

The humpback whale breathes out through a pair of blowholes, located behind a ridge called a splashguard. This helps prevent water from entering the blowholes when the whale is blowing.

17

# Whale Brain and Senses

A whale controls its body through its nervous system. The brain is the control center, carrying out functions automatically, but also acting upon information supplied by the senses. The size of whale brains varies, according to the animal's size. However, dolphins have much bigger brains for their size. Hearing is by far a whale's most important sense. They pick up sounds with tiny ears located just behind the eyes.

▲ EYES

Compared with its large body, a whale's eyes are tiny. It can see quite well when it is on the surface and often lifts its head out of the water to look around.

Did you know? A sperm whale's brain is five times the size of a human's.

◀ CLOSE ENCOUNTERS

A group of Atlantic spotted dolphins swims closely together in the seas around the Bahama Islands. Like most other cetaceans, the dolphins often nudge one another and stroke each other with their flippers and tail. Touch plays a very important part in dolphin society, especially in courtship.

◄ SLAP HAPPY

A humpback whale slapping its tail, or lob-tailing, a favorite pastime for great whales. Lob-tailing creates a noise like a gunshot in the air, but, more importantly, it will make a loud report underwater. All the other whales in the area will be able to hear the noise.

*Cupids and Dolphins*

*In this Roman mosaic, cupids and dolphins gambol together. In Roman mythology, Cupid was the god of love. Roman artists were inspired by the dolphin's intelligence and gentleness. They regarded them as sacred creatures.*

◄ BRAINY DOLPHIN?

Some dolphins, such as the bottlenose, have a brain that is much the same size as our own. It is quite a complex brain with many folds.

► IN TRAINING

A bottlenose dolphin is shown with its trainer. This species has a particularly large brain for its size. It can be easily trained and has a good memory. It can observe other animals and learn to mimic their behavior in a short amount of time. It is also good at solving problems, a sign of intelligence.

# Sounds and Songs

Whales use sounds to communicate with one another, and to find their food. Baleen whales use low-pitched sounds, which have been picked up by underwater microphones as moans, grunts and snores. The toothed whales make higher-pitched sounds, picked up as squeaks, creaks or whistles. Whales also use high-pitched clicks when hunting. They send out beams of sound, which are reflected by objects in their path, such as fish. The whale picks up the reflected sound, or echo, and figures out the object's location. This is called echolocation.

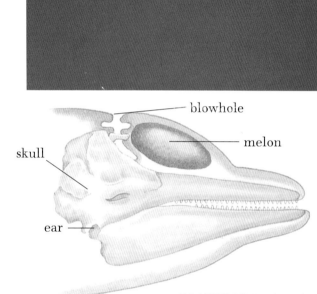

blowhole

melon

skull

ear

#### ◄ ECHO SOUNDINGS
The Amazon river dolphin hunts by echolocation. It sends out up to 80 high-pitched clicks per second. The sound transmits in a beam from a bulge on top of its head. All toothed whales and dolphins hunt in this way.

#### ▲ MAKING WAVES
A dolphin vibrates the air in its nasal passages to make high-pitched sound waves, which are focused into a beam by the melon—a bulge on its head. The sound beam transmits into the water.

#### ► SEA CANARIES
A group of belugas, or white whales, swims in a bay in Canada. Belugas' voices can clearly be heard above the surface. This is why they are known as sea canaries. They also produce high-pitched sounds we cannot hear, which they use for echolocation.

### ◄ SUPER SONGSTER

This male humpback whale is heading for the breeding grounds where the females are gathering. The male starts singing long and complicated songs. This may be to attract a mate, or to warn other males away from its patch. The sound can carry for 18 mi. or more.

### ▼ LONG SONGS

This is a voice print of a humpback whale's song, picked up by an underwater microphone. It shows complex musical phrases and melodies. Humpback whales often continue singing for a day or more, repeating the same song.

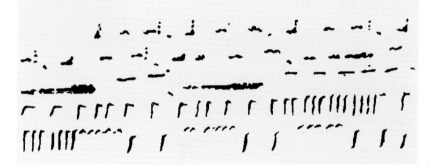

### ▼ SOUND ECHOES

A sperm whale can locate a giant squid more than a mile away by transmitting pulses of sound waves into the water and listening. The echo is picked up by the teeth in its lower jaw and the vibrations are sent along the jaw to the ear.

Did you know? A dolphin picks up sounds through its lower jaw.

### ◄ ALIEN GREETINGS

The songs of the humpback whale travel not only through earth's oceans, but also far out into space. They are among the recorded typical sounds of our world that are being carried by the two Voyager space probes. These probes are now many millions of miles away from earth and are on their way to the stars.

21

# Feeding Habits

**▲ CRUNCHY KRILL**

These crustaceans, known as krill, form the diet of many baleen whales. Measuring up to 3 in. long, they swim in vast schools, often covering an area of several square miles. Most krill are found in Antarctic waters.

Most baleen whales feed by taking mouthfuls of seawater containing fish and tiny shrimp-like creatures called krill or plankton, as well as algae, jellyfish, worms and so on. The whale closes its mouth and lifts its tongue, forcing water out through the bristly baleen plates on the upper jaw. The baleen acts like a sieve and holds back the food, which the whale then swallows. Toothed whales feed mainly on fish and squid. They find their prey by echolocation.

**◄ PLOWING**

A gray whale plows into the seabed, stirring up sand and ooze. It dislodges tiny crustaceans, called amphipods, and gulps them down. Gray whales feed mostly in summer in the Arctic before they migrate south.

**◄ SKIM FEEDING**

With its mouth open, a southern right whale filters tiny crustaceans, called copepods, out of the water with its baleen. It eats up to two tons of these plankton daily. It eats so much because of its huge size—up to 80 tons. Usually right whales feed alone, but if food is plentiful, several will feed cruising side by side.

**◄ SUCCULENT SQUID**

Squid is the sperm whale's favorite food and is eaten by other toothed whales and dolphins as well. Squid are mollusks, in the same animal order as snails and octopuses. Unlike octopuses, they have eight arms and two tentacles, and are called decapods (meaning ten feet). Squid swim together in dense schools, many thousand strong.

**◄ TOOTHY SMILE**

A Ganges river dolphin has more than 100 teeth. The front ones are very long. Ganges river dolphins eat mainly fish, and also take shrimp and crab. They usually feed at night and find their prey by echolocation.

*Did you know? A blue whale eats nearly 2,200 lbs of krill in a single meal.*

**► LUNCH**

Belugas feed on squid and small fish, which are in plentiful supply in the icy ocean. Unlike common dolphins, belugas do not have many teeth. They may simply suck prey into their mouths. Many beaked whales, which also feed on squid, have no teeth suitable for clutching prey.

**▲ HUNT THE SQUID**

The sperm whale is the largest toothed whale, notable for its huge head and tiny lower jaw. It hunts the giant squid that live in waters around 6,500 ft deep. At that depth, in total darkness, it hunts its prey by echolocation.

23

# Focus on

1 A killer whale will go hunting by itself if it chances upon a likely victim, such as this lone sea lion. This hungry whale has spotted the sea lion splashing in the surf at the water's edge. With powerful strokes of its tail, it surges toward its intended prey. The whale's tall dorsal fin shows that it is a fully-grown male.

Among the toothed whales, the killer whale, or orca, is the master predator. It feeds on a wider variety of prey than any other whale. It bites and tears its prey to pieces with its fearsome teeth and may also batter them with its powerful tail. It is the only whale to eat warm-blooded prey. Fortunately, there is no record of a killer whale ever attacking human beings in the wild. As well as fish and squid, a killer whale will hunt seals, penguins, dolphins and porpoises. It may even attack large baleen whales many times its size. Killer whales live in family groups, or pods. They often go hunting together, which greatly improves their chance of success.

2 The sea lion seems totally unaware of what is happening but, in any case, it is nearly helpless in the shallow water. The killer whale is scraping the shore as it homes in for the kill.

# Killer Whales

**3** Suddenly the killer's head bursts out of the water, and its jaws gape open. Its sharp teeth, curving inward and backward, are exposed. It is ready to sink them into its sea lion prey. The killer whale may have fewer teeth than most toothed whales, but they are large and very strong.

**4** Now the killer snaps its jaws shut, clamping the sea lion in a vice-like grip. With its prey struggling helplessly, it slides back into deep water to eat its fill. Killer whales sometimes almost beach themselves when they lunge after prey but, helped by the surf, they usually manage to wriggle their way back into the sea.

The humpback whale usually scoops up water as it lunges forward and upward to feed. Grooves in its throat lets the mouth expand to take in tons of water containing food, which it filters through its baleen plates. This way of lunge-feeding is typical of the baleen whales known as the rorquals, which also include the blue, fin, sei and minke whales. Before lunge-feeding, humpbacks may blow a circle of bubbles around the fish. The bubbles act like a net to stop the fish from escaping.

## ON THE LOOKOUT

A humpback whale spy-hops in the feeding grounds of Alaska. It is looking for signs of schools of fish, such as cod. In the Northern Hemisphere, humpbacks feed mainly on fish. The Southern Hemisphere humpbacks feed mainly on plankton, such as krill.

## FORWARD LUNGE

Once in the middle of a school, the humpback opens its mouth and lunges forward. The throat grooves expand as water rushes in. It uses its tongue and cheek muscles to force the water through its baleen plates, leaving the fish behind in its mouth.

# Lunging for Lunch

**UPWARD LUNGE**
Here, the humpback is using a different technique. It sinks below the surface and then flicks its tail to help it to shoot upward again. With mouth gaping open, it lunges at the fish from below.

**RING OF BUBBLES**
The surface of the sea is erupting with a ring of frothy bubbles. Unseen, beneath the water, one or more humpback whales swim in circles, letting out air as they do so.

**BUBBLE NETTING**
The circle of bubbles rises to the surface from the whales circling under the water. It forms a kind of net around a school of fish. The whales then swim up to the surface, mouths gaping, to engulf the netted prey.

27

# Swimming

All whales are superb swimmers. All parts of the whale's body help it move through the water. The driving force comes from the tail fin, or flukes. Using very powerful muscles in the rear third of its body, the whale beats its tail up and down, and the whole body bends. It uses its pectoral fins, or flippers, near the front of the body to steer with. The body itself is streamlined and smooth to help it slip through the water easily. The body can change shape slightly to keep the water flowing smoothly around it. Little ridges under the skin help as well.

## ▲ STEERING

Among whales, the humpback has by far the longest front flippers. As well as for steering, it uses its flippers for slapping the water. Flipper-slapping seems to be a form of communication.

## ◄ TAIL POWER

The tail flukes of a gray whale rise into the air before it dives. Whales move their broad tails up and down to drive themselves through the water

## ▼ MASSIVE FIN

The dorsal fin of a killer whale projects high into the air. The animal is a swift swimmer, and the fin helps keep its body well balanced. The killer whale has such a large dorsal fin that some experts believe it may help to regulate their body temperature, or even be used in courtship. Most whales and dolphins have a dorsal fin, although some only have a raised hump.

Did you know? A killer whale can swim up to 40 miles per hour.

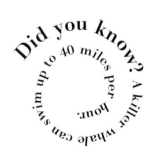

### ◄ STREAMLINING

Atlantic spotted dolphins' bodies are beautifully streamlined—shaped so that they slip easily through the water when they move. The dolphin's body is long and rounded, broad in front and becoming narrower toward the tail. Apart from the dorsal fin and flippers, nothing projects from its body. It has no external ears or rear limbs.

### ▼ HOW A DOLPHIN SWIMS

Dolphins beat their tail flukes up and down by means of the powerful muscles near the tail. The flukes force the water backward at each stroke. As the water is forced back, the dolphin's body is forced forward. Its other fins help guide it through the water. They do not provide propulsion.

### ◄ SMOOTH SKINNED

This bottlenose dolphin is tailwalking—supporting itself by powerful thrusts of its tail. Unlike most mammals, it has no covering of hair or hair follicles—the dimples in the skin from which the hair grows. Its smooth skin helps the dolphin's body slip through the water.

### ▼ HOW A FISH SWIMS

It is mainly the tail that provides the power for a fish to swim. The tail has vertical fins, unlike the horizontal fins of the dolphin. It swims by beating its tail and body from side to side.

29

# *Focus on*

Most whales feed beneath the surface, some often diving deep to reach their food. We can usually identify the species of whale from the way it prepares to dive, or sound. The sperm whale, for example, is one of the species that lifts its tail high into the air before it descends into the ocean. It is the deepest diver of all the whales, sometimes descending to more than a mile in search of squid. It can stay under water for an hour or more before it has to come up for air. As in other whales, its lungs collapse when it dives. It is thought that the great mass of oil in its head helps the whale when diving and surfacing.

1 Two sperm whales swim at the surface. The one on the right is preparing to dive. Its head is in the air, and it fills its lungs with air in a series of blows. The sperm whale's blow projects forward, as in no other whale.

2 The diving whale lashes its tail and accelerates through the water, creating a foaming wake. Now the whale starts the dive, thrusting its bulbous head down and arching its back steeply. The rounded hump on its back rises high into the air. The lumpy knuckles behind the hump become visible as the body arches over.

# Diving

**3** As the whale's head goes under, the oil in its head freezes and becomes heavier on the way down, then melts and becomes lighter again on the way up. If it is going to make a deep dive, the whale may not take another breath for more than an hour.

**4** Soon the body disappears with just the tail flukes poking out of the water. The body is now in a vertical position, and that is how it remains as the whale dives swiftly into the deep. Descending at speeds of more than 490ft per minute, it is soon in darkness, scanning its surroundings by beams of sound for the squid on which it feeds.

# Social Life

Every day we meet, work, play and communicate with other people. We are sociable animals. Some whales are also sociable and live together. Sperm whales live in groups of up to about 50. A group may be a breeding school of females and young or a bachelor school of young males. Older male sperm whales live alone, except in the breeding season. Beluga whales often live in groups of several hundred. Baleen whales are not as sociable. They move alone or in small groups, probably because of their huge appetite—they could not find enough food if they lived close together.

▲ **HERD INSTINCT**

Beluga whales gather together in very large groups, or herds, and they mostly stay in these herds for life. Many of the animals in this group, pictured in the Canadian Arctic, have calves. These can be recognized, not only by their smaller size, but also by their darker skin color.

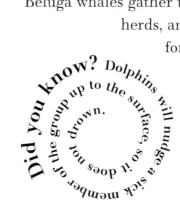

**Did you know?** Dolphins will nudge a sick member of the group up to the surface, so it does not drown.

▼ **NOSEY ORCAS**

Two killer whales, or orcas, spy-hop in Antarctic waters. They rise out of the water together, as if on a signal. They are members of the same pod, which stays together all their lives. The bonds between the animals are very strong. This helps them coordinate their activities, especially when hunting for food.

**◄ STAYING CLOSE**

Two Atlantic spotted dolphins swim with their young. The young's spots will not start to appear until the animals are about a year old. As with many other species, the young stay very close to their parents most of the time.

**▼ HUMAN CONTACT**

A bottlenose dolphin swims alongside a boy. These dolphins live in social groups, but lone outcasts, or animals that have become separated from their group, often approach humans.

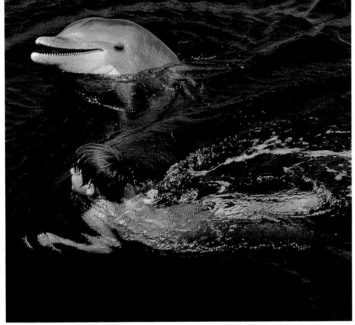

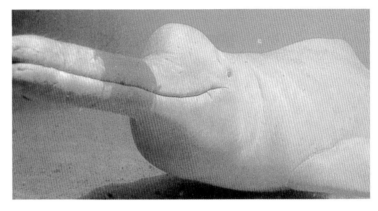

**▲ SOLITARY SWIMMER**

An Amazon river dolphin rests on the river bed. It spends most of its life alone, or with just one other. This solitary behavior is typical of river dolphins, but not typical of most whales and ocean dolphins.

**► PILOT ERROR**

These long-finned pilot whales are stranded on a beach. Pilot whales usually live in large groups, with strong bonds between group members. One whale may strand itself on a beach. The others may try to help it and get stranded themselves.

33

# The Mating Game

Whales mate at certain times of year. Baleen whales mate during the late autumn after the whales have migrated to their warm-water breeding grounds. One whale will mate a number of times with different partners. Several males may attempt to maneuver a female into a mating position. Often the males fight each other for the chance to mate. Male narwhals even fence with their long tusks. But mating behavior can also be gentle, with the males and females caressing one another with their flippers.

▲ WHITE WEDDING
A pair of belugas shows interest in each other. Males and females spend the year in separate groups, only mixing in the mating season. They mate and calve in bays in the far north.

◄ LOVE SONG
Whales attract mates by body language and sound. This humpback can pinpoint another's position, and perhaps exchange messages, over great distances.

◄ MATING TIFFS
Two gray whales court in the winter breeding grounds off Baja California, Mexico. Usually, a group of males fights for the right to mate with a female, causing commotion in the water. The female might mate many times with them.

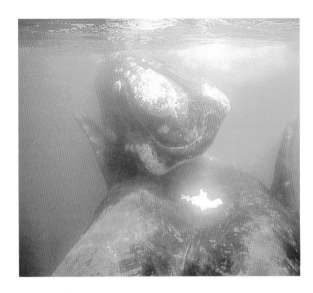

◄ **ROLL OVER**

Courtship for these southern right whales is nearly over. The male *(top)* has succeeded in getting the female to roll over on her back and is moving into the mating position.

***The Fabulous Unicorn***

*In the breeding season, male narwhals fight each other using their long tusks, which often break. Long ago, when these small whales were little known, people found the tusks and wondered what kind of creature they came from. This may have led to the idea of the unicorn, a horse-like beast with a long spiral horn (like the narwhal's) on its forehead.*

◄ **BELLY TO BELLY**

A pair of southern right whales mates, belly to belly. The male has inserted his long penis into the female to inject his sperm. Usually, the male's penis stays hidden in the body behind a genital slit. It will be nine months or more before the female gives birth to a single calf.

▼ **BIG BABY**

A sperm whale calf snuggles up to its mother. A calf might measure up to 14 ft long when born, nearly 15 months after mating took place. The mother feeds it for a year or more, leaving it only to dive deep for food.

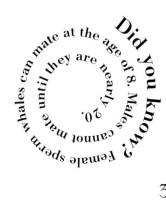

Did you know? Female sperm whales can mate at the age of 8. Males cannot mate until they are nearly 20.

# Focus on

**BIRTHDAY**
A bottlenose dolphin gives birth. The baby is born tail-first. This birth is taking place near the bottom at an aquarium. In the wild, birth takes place close to the surface so the baby can surface quickly and start breathing.

After mating, the female whale becomes pregnant and a baby whale starts to grow inside her body. After about a year, the calf is ready to be born. By now it can weigh, in the case of the blue whale, up to 2.7 tons. The first thing the calf must do is take a breath, and the mother or another whale may help it to the surface. Soon it finds one of the mother's nipples to suck the rich milk in her mammary glands (breasts). It suckles for several months until it learns to take solid food such as fish. Mother and calf may spend most of the time alone, or join nursery schools with other mothers and calves.

**SUCKLING**
A beluga mother suckles her young under water. Her fatty milk is very nutritious, and the calf grows rapidly. It will drink milk for up to two years. At birth the calf's body is dark gray, but it slowly lightens as the calf matures.

# Bringing Up Baby

**Did you know?** The calves of baleen whales stop breast feeding after about 9 months—much sooner than toothed whale calves.

## AT PLAY

A young Atlantic spotted dolphin and its mother play together, twisting, turning, rolling and touching each other with their flippers. During play, the young dolphin learns the skills it will need later in life when it has to fend for itself. The youngster is darker than its mother and has no spots. These do not start to appear until it is about a year old.

## TOGETHERNESS

A humpback whale calf sticks closely to its mother as she swims slowly in Hawaiian waters. The slipstream, or water flow, created by the mother's motion helps pull it along. For the first few months of its life, it will not stray far from its mother's side.

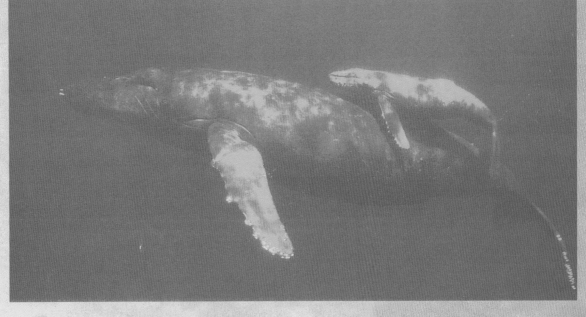

# Having Fun

Dolphins have long delighted people with their acrobatic antics. They somersault, ride the bow waves of boats and go surfing. Dusky and spinner dolphins are particularly lively. Some antics have a purpose, such as sending signals to other dolphins. But often the animals seem to perform just for fun. In most animal species only the young play. In whale and dolphin society, adults play too. Southern right whales play a sailing game. They hang in the water with their heads down and tails in the air. The tails act like sails and catch the wind, and they are blown along.

**▲ PLAYFUL PAIR**

Two Atlantic spotted dolphins jostle as they play with a sea fan. Dolphins spend much of their time playing, especially the younger ones. They make up games, using anything they can find. Their games can last for hours.

**▼ JUMPING FOR JOY**

A pair of bottlenose dolphins leaps high, leaving the water together, as if they have rehearsed their act. They seem to jump for joy, but their behavior may have a social function within their family group.

## ▶ PORPOISING ON PURPOSE

A group of long-snouted spinner dolphins goes porpoising, taking long, low leaps as they swim. They churn the water behind them into foam. Many dolphins practice porpoising, in order to travel fast on the surface.

*Did you know? Killer whales like brushing against each other as they swim at high speed.*

## ◀ RIDING THE WAKE

A Pacific white-sided dolphin surfs the waves. This is one of the most acrobatic of the dolphins. It is often seen bow-riding in front of boats. Other species of dolphins also like to ride in the waves left in the wake of passing boats.

*Did you know? The rough skin on a porpoise's back may be for giving calves piggy-back rides.*

## ▶ AQUATIC ACROBAT

This dusky dolphin is throwing itself high into the air. It twists and turns, spins and performs somersaults. This behavior is like a roll call—to check that every dolphin in the group is present and ready to go hunting. The behavior is repeated after hunting to gather the group together once more.

*Did you know? A dolphin may play cat and mouse with its prey before eating it.*

# Focus on

A whale leaps from the sea and crashes back to the surface in a shower of spray. This activity, called breaching, is common among humpbacks. Some may breach up to 200 times in succession. When one animal starts breaching, others follow suit. Whales put on other displays as well, including slapping their flippers and tail on the surface. These activities could, like breaching, be some form of signaling. Spy-hopping is another activity, often done to look for signs of fish to eat.

## BREACHING

Propelled by powerful thrusts of its tail, the humpback launches its vast bulk into the air, twisting as it does so. For a creature weighing up to 30 tons, this is no mean feat. As breaching ends, it crashes back to the surface with a splash. This time it lands on its back, with one of its flippers up in the air.

## FLIPPER-FLOPPING

The humpback swims on the surface, raising one flipper in the air. It rolls over and slaps the flipper on the water several times, perhaps to warn off rivals. Its flipper-flopping is noisy because its flippers are so large.

# Whales on Display

### WHAT A FLUKE!

The humpback raises its tail in the air during the display known as lob-tailing or tail-slapping. The tail is also exposed when the whale is about to dive, behavior called fluking. It is easy to tell if a humpback is lob-tailing or fluking. In fluking, the tail disappears below the surface quietly.

### LOB-TAILING

In lob-tailing, the tail slaps on the water with a noise like a gunshot. The only other time a humpback shows its flukes is when it is about to go on a deep dive.

### SPY-HOPPING

The humpback on the right of the picture is spy-hopping. It positions itself vertically in the water and pokes out its head until its eyes are showing. Then it has a good look around. The other humpback here is doing the opposite, poking out its tail, ready to lob-tail.

# Where Whales are Found

Whales are found in all the world's oceans. Some kinds live all over, while others are found only in a certain area. They may stay in the same place all year long, or migrate from one area to another with the seasons. Some whales stick to shallow coastal areas, others prefer deep waters. Some live in the cool northern or southern parts of the world. Others are more at home in tropical regions near the equator. Some species even live in rivers.

### ▼ OCEAN WANDERER

A humpback whale surfaces to blow while swimming at Cape Cod off the northeast coast of North America. In winter, the humpback feeds in high latitudes. It migrates to low latitudes to breed during the summer.

### ▲ MUDDY WATERS

The mud-laden waters of the Amazon River in South America are the habitat of the Amazon river dolphin. Here, one shows off its teeth. This species ranges along the Amazon and its tributaries.

**Did you know?** Some dolphins come and go between salt water and fresh water.

### ◄ WORLDWIDE ORCA

Among ice-floes in the Arctic Ocean, a killer whale, or orca, hunts for prey. Killer whales are found in all the oceans. They live in coastal areas but may venture out to the open ocean. They also swim in the surf along the shore, and may beach to snatch their prey.

▶ **SNOW WHITE**
These belugas, or white whales, are in Hudson Bay, Canada. These cold-water animals live around coasts in the far north of North America, Europe and Asia. They venture into estuaries and even up rivers. In winter they hunt in the pack ice in the Arctic.

◀ **TROPICAL MELONS**
A pod of melon-headed whales is shown swimming in the Pacific Ocean. These creatures prefer warm waters and are found in subtropical and tropical regions in both the Northern and Southern Hemispheres. They generally stay in deep water, keeping well away from land.

▶ **WIDE RANGER**
A bottlenose dolphin lunges through the surf in the sunny Bahamas. This animal is one of the most wide-ranging of the dolphins, being found in temperate to tropical waters in both the Northern and Southern Hemispheres. It is also found in enclosed seas such as the Mediterranean and Red Sea. Mostly it stays in coastal waters. When bottlenose dolphins migrate to warmer areas, they lose weight. When they return to colder climes, their blubber increases again.

43

# Migration

Gray whales spend the summer months feeding in the Arctic Ocean. Many of the females are pregnant. Before winter comes, the whales head south toward Mexico for warmer waters, where the females will give birth to their calves. In the warmer climate, the calves stand a better chance of surviving. Mating takes place around late summer. When spring comes, the grays head north to the Arctic. Their annual journey between feeding and breeding grounds involves a round trip of some 12,400 miles. The humpbacks take part in long migrations too. Most of the other large rorquals and the right whales seem to undergo similar migrations.

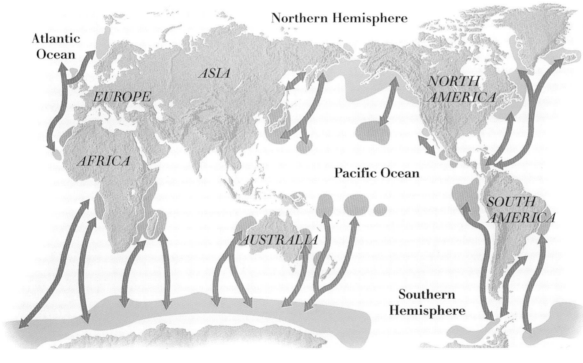

**Migration**
*This map shows the routes taken by humpback whales during their annual migrations between their summer feeding and winter breeding grounds. There are at least three main groups, two in the Northern and one in the Southern Hemisphere.*

**KEY TO MAP**

 breeding grounds    feeding grounds

**◂ SUMMER FEEDING**
Two Southern Hemisphere humpbacks feed in the Antarctic Ocean during the summer months. This is when the krill and other plankton they feed on thrive. The whales have taken huge mouthfuls of water, which they sieve for plankton using the baleen on their upper jaws.

## ▼ RIGHT LOCATION

The tail fluke of a southern right whale is thrust into the air as the whale sails. This whale is one of a group of right whales in winter breeding grounds off the coast of Argentina. By summer the whales will have returned south to feed in the Antarctic Ocean.

Did you know? Gray whales make longer migrations than any other mammal.

## ▲ WINTER BREEDING

It is early winter, and two humpbacks have migrated north from the Antarctic to a shallow bay on the coast of eastern Australia. A large group of humpbacks will mate here and, about 12 months later, the females will give birth.

## ▼ MATING GRAYS

In the winter breeding grounds of Baja California, a gray whale surfaces. They spend about three months in the region, where mating and (two years later) births take place.

# High and Dry

Dead whales are often found washed up, or stranded, on the beach. Live whales are sometimes found too, particularly open ocean species, such as sperm whales. Some live whales probably get stranded when they become ill. Others get stranded when they lose their sense of direction. Whales are thought to find their way using the earth's magnetism as a kind of map. Any change in the magnetism may cause them to turn the wrong way and head for the shore. Mass strandings also take place, with scores of whales left helpless. This happens particularly among sociable species, such as the pilot whales.

*Did you know? It is unknown why rescued whales will often swim back and get stranded again.*

▲ BEACHED DOLPHIN
This Atlantic white-sided dolphin is stranded on a beach in the Orkney Islands. The dolphins usually travel in big groups, so mass strandings also occur.

▲ WAITING FOR THE TIDE
People come to the aid of more than 60 stranded long-finned pilot whales on the beach in New Zealand. They cover the whales to prevent sunburn and throw water over them to keep their skin moist.

### ◀ RARE STRANDING

Marine biologists examine a stranded Stejneger's beaked whale. Beaked whales are among the least known of all the cetaceans. Most of our knowledge about them comes from occasional strandings. Several beaked whales, such as this one, have a large tooth protruding from the jaws.

Did you know? Whales stranded in Great Britain belong to the monarch.

### ▶ IN THE SHALLOWS

Three belugas became stranded in shallow water as the tide went out. Polar bears may attack when they are beached. Belugas rarely become completely stranded, and usually survive until the tide comes in again.

### ▼ BIG FIN

A huge fin whale has become beached on a mudflat. This animal is dead, but even if it were alive, it would be impossible to return to the water. When a whale of this size is not supported by water, its internal organs collapse. Scientists examine stranded bodies to learn about whales.

# Gray and Right Whales

Gray whales and the three species of right whale, including the bowhead, are all filter-feeders with baleen plates in their upper jaws. The bowhead has the longest baleen of all, while the gray whale has short baleen. Unlike most baleen whales, the gray whale feeds mainly on the seabed. It is found only in the Northern Hemisphere, but there are right whales in both hemispheres. Right whales were named by whalers because they were the right whales to catch for their high yields of oil and baleen. They swam slowly, could be approached easily and floated when dead.

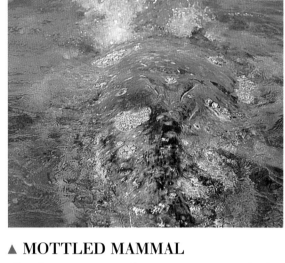

### ▲ MOTTLED MAMMAL

The long, narrow head of a gray whale breaks the surface. Its closed blowholes are in the middle of the picture. The head is covered here and there with clusters of barnacles and lice. This, together with lighter body patches, gives the animal a mottled appearance.

### ◄ LIVELY LOB

Near the coast of Argentina in South America, a southern right whale is lob-tailing. In seconds, its tail will crash down on the surface with a smack that will echo off the cliffs on the shore. The noise will be heard by other whales, many miles away. Right whales often lob-tail and also do headstands, waving their tails in the air.

### ▲ WHITE CHIN

A bowhead whale thrusts its head out of the water, exposing its unique white chin, covered with black patches. The skin is smooth, with no growths like those on the skin of the northern and southern right whales.

**Did you know?** We know a lot about gray whales because they stay in shallow waters near the coast.

### ◄ BEARDED

A southern right whale cruises in the South Atlantic. One distinctive feature of this whale is the deeply curved jawline. Another is its beard and "bonnet." These are large growths on the whale's chin and nose, which become infested with barnacles.

### ◄ HAIRY MONSTER

The northern right whale lives in the North Atlantic. Whalers used to call the hard crusty skin on its head a "bonnet" or rock garden. Lice and barnacles live on this skin, which can grow enormous. Right whales are the hairiest of all whales, keeping more hair after birth than other cetaceans. It even grows facial hair!

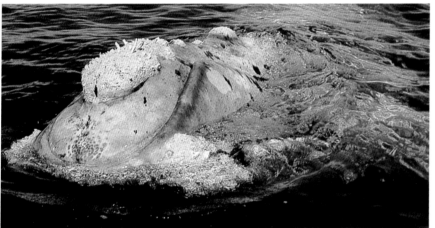

**Did you know?** You can tell a gray whale by its unique long, very narrow head.

### ► BRISTLY JAWS

A gray whale opens its mouth, showing the baleen plates on its upper jaw. The baleen is quite short, stiff and coarse. The whale uses it to filter out the tiny creatures it digs out of the seabed when feeding. Gray whales are not shy and sometimes swim up to the boats of whale-watchers.

# Rorquals

The rorquals are a family of baleen whales that includes the largest creature ever to live, the blue whale. They are named after the grooves on their throat—the word rorqual means a furrow. All rorquals, except the humpback, have a long streamlined body with a sharp nose and a dorsal fin set well back. They can swim at up to 18 mph. The humpback is a slower swimmer with a chunkier body. It has bumpy flippers and a hump in front of the dorsal fin. It is famous for the songs it sings. The minke whale is the smallest rorqual. Bryde's whale lives mainly in tropical and subtropical waters, while the other rorquals often venture into colder waters as well, even venturing into polar waters in the summer.

## ▼ TINY MINKE

The minke whale grows to only about one-third of the size of the blue whale and never exceeds 10 tons in weight. It has a slim snout and a curved dorsal fin. Its flippers are short and can be marked with a broad white band.

## ▲ WHALE WITH A HUMP

This picture of a humpback whale shows the feature that gives it its name very well. Its small dorsal fin sits on top of a pronounced hump on its back. This profile view of the animal also shows the prominent splash guard on its head in front of the blowholes.

Did you know? Humpback whales can live to age 95.

## ▼ BUMPY FLIPPER

A humpback whale swims on the surface, with one of its flippers up in the air like a boat sail. The flippers of the humpback are by far the most distinctive of all the whales. They are sturdy and very long—up to a third of the length of the whale's body. The flippers have bumps along their front edge.

flipper

**◄ BIG GULP**

A blue whale feeds in Californian waters. It has taken in a mouthful of water containing thousands of the tiny shrimp-like krill it feeds on. The grooves on its throat that allow its mouth to expand can be clearly seen. A blue whale typically has between 60 and 90 of these grooves.

**► DRIPPING FLUKES**

A blue whale is fluking, with its tail flukes rising out of the water before the animal dives. Among rorquals, only blue and humpback whales expose their flukes before diving. The humpback's tail flukes are quite different. They are bumpy at the rear edges and have white markings on the underside.

*Did you know?*
*A blue whale's heart is about the size of a small car.*

**◄ SEI WHALE**

The sei whale can be found in most of the oceans. It feeds in the cool Arctic or Antarctic waters during the summer and migrates to warmer waters in the winter to breed. With a length of up to about 60 ft, it is slightly larger than the similar looking Bryde's whale.

51

# Sperm and White Whales

The sperm and the white whales are two families of toothed whales. The sperm whale and dwarf and pygmy sperm whales have an organ in their head called the spermaceti organ, which is filled with wax. The wax may help the animals when they dive and may play a part in focusing the sound waves they use for echolocation. The sperm whale and the two white whales (the beluga and the narwhal) have no dorsal fin. The sperm whale has teeth only on its lower jaw. The beluga has up to 20 teeth in each of its jaws, but the narwhal has only two. In the male narwhal, one of the teeth grows into a long spiral tusk, measuring up to 10 ft.

◀ **BABY EYES**

The eye of a sperm whale calf. Like all whales, the sperm whale has tiny eyes compared with those of most other mammals. But this does not matter because when the whale dives to feed, it descends deep into the ocean where light never reaches. It depends on its superb echolocation system to find its prey.

**Did you know?** perfume is made from the wax made in sperm whales' guts.

**Did you know?** A sperm whale can dive as deep as 9,800 ft in search of squid.

◀ **LOOKING AROUND**

A beluga raises its head above the water to look around—they are inquisitive creatures. Belugas have short heads with rounded bulges called melons. They also have noticeable necks, allowing them to turn their heads, and a wide range of facial expressions—they often appear to be smiling.

◄ COW AND CALF
A sperm whale cow swims with her calf. Cows suckle their young for at least two years in a nursery group with other cows and calves. This picture shows the sperm whale's unique body shape, with its huge blunt snout. The sperm whale does not have a dorsal fin, just a triangular lump on its back.

► HIGH SOCIETY
This pod of belugas is swimming in Arctic waters off the coast of Canada. Belugas are usually found in such pods because they are very social animals. Note the typical body characteristics, including broad stubby flippers and the lack of a dorsal fin.

▼ LONG IN THE TOOTH
In freezing Arctic waters a male narwhal comes to the surface to blow, its long tusk raised. The tusk has a spiral shape and can be up to 10 ft long. It is one of the narwhal's two teeth. A small number of males produce twin tusks.

tusk

▲ COLOR, SHAPE AND WEIGHT
The narwhal's stocky body is much like that of the beluga. Both grow up to about 16 ft long and weigh up to 3,300 lbs. The main difference is in the color. Whereas the beluga is white, the narwhal is mostly a mottled dark and light gray.

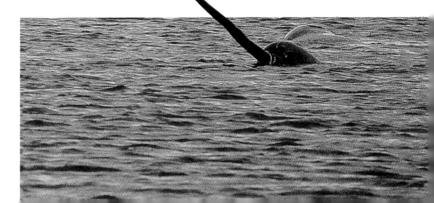

# Beaked, Pilot and Killer Whales

Beaked whales are named after their beak, which is much like that of many kinds of dolphin. Unlike dolphins, they have hardly any teeth—most have just two. Beaked whales live mainly in the deep ocean, and little is known about them. Pilot and killer whales are better known. They are part of the dolphin family and, like many dolphins, tend to live in quite large groups. Because pilot whales and killer whales are mostly black, they are often called blackfish. The killer whale is the largest and best known of the family and is a fierce predator.

▲ **A TELLING TAIL**
A killer whale lob-tails. Its tail is black on top but mainly white underneath, with a distinct notch in the middle. Note also the pointed tips of the flukes.

◄ **KILLER LEAP**
A killer whale leaps high into the air while breaching in Alaskan waters. The whale may twist and turn before it falls back to the surface with a resounding splash. Look at this killer whale's broad paddle-shaped flippers. The size and shape of the flippers and the dorsal fin mark this specimen as a male.

Did you know? Killer whales have never been known to attack humans in the wild.

## ◄ CRUISING PILOT

The short-finned pilot whale has a broad, bulbous head, and is for this reason sometimes called the pothead whale. It has sickle-shaped flippers and a curved dorsal fin. This pilot whale prefers tropical and subtropical regions. The long-finned pilot whale is similar, but with slightly longer flippers, and lives in the Southern Hemisphere in both cool and warm waters.

## ► WHITE LIPS

A pod of melon-headed whales swims close together. One of them is spy-hopping, and shows its melon-shaped head. Note its white lips.

## ◄ SLEEK LINES

Note the streamlined body of the killer whale as it comes out of the water while performing at Sea World in California. The picture shows its white patches behind the eye and at the side, and the white chin. There is a grayish saddle patch behind the dorsal fin.

## ▼ FALSE TEETH

A false killer whale spy-hops. False killer whales have as many as 20 teeth in each jaw. They do not look much like the killer whale and are smaller. They have no white patches and their heads are more slender.

## ► LONER

A beaked whale swims alone. Most spend a lot of time alone or with one or two others. They prefer deep waters, and some species dive very deep indeed.

# Oceanic Dolphins

Dolphins are the most common of all cetaceans. They are swift swimmers and have sleek, streamlined bodies with, usually, a prominent dorsal fin. They have dark gray backs and white or pale gray bellies. Many dolphins have contrasting stripes along the sides. About half the dolphin species have long beaks, and as many as 250 teeth. The rest have short beaks and fewer teeth. Dolphins can be found in most oceans, but not usually in the cold waters of far northern or far southern regions. Most are highly sociable, some traveling together in groups of hundreds.

**◄ STRIKING STRIPES**
Distinctive black and white striped bodies tell us that these two animals are southern right whale-dolphins. The back is jet black, while the beak, forehead, belly and flippers are white.

**▼ PORPOISING DOLPHINS**
A group of common dolphins is porpoising—taking long, low leaps. They have a long beak and yellow markings on their sides. The dark skin on the upper back looks like a saddle. This is why it is also called the saddleback dolphin.

**Did you know?** Dolphins make loud noises when hunting to panic fish into herding together.

## ◄ GREAT LEAPERS

Two bottlenose dolphins launch themselves with great energy several yards into the air. Their bodies are mainly gray in color. The head of the bottlenose dolphin is more rounded than that of most other beaked dolphins.

## ► BLUNT HEADS

A group of Risso's dolphins is easy to recognize by their blunt heads and tall dorsal fins. Their bodies are mainly gray on the back and sides. The color becomes paler with age, and some old adults are nearly all white.

## ▼ PALE FACE

The odd-looking Irrawaddy dolphin has a rounded head and a distinct neck, much like the beluga. Its flippers are large and curved. It is found in rivers and estuaries, as well as coastal waters from south of India as far as northern Australia.

### Dolphin Rescue

*An old Greek tale tells of a famed poet and musician named Arion. After a concert tour, sailors on the ship that was taking him home set out to kill him for his money. They granted his request to sing a final song. Then he jumped overboard. He did not drown because a dolphin, attracted by his beautiful song, carried him to the shore.*

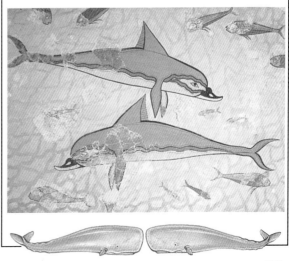

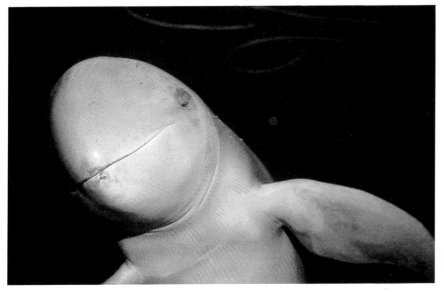

# Porpoises and River Dolphins

Porpoises look much like dolphins, yet they form a separate cetacean family. They are smaller than most dolphins and do not have a typical dolphin beak. Their teeth are different, being spade-like instead of cone-shaped. Most porpoises are shy. The rare river dolphins form a separate family. They have a long slender beak and a rounded forehead. Their flexible neck allows their head to turn, unlike oceanic dolphins. In the muddy waters where they mostly live, they use echolocation rather than their poor eyesight to find the fish and other creatures they feed on.

### ▲ BEAKED BOTO

The Amazon river dolphin, or boto, has the typical long beak of the river dolphins. Its color varies from pale bluish-gray to pink. It has no dorsal fin, just a fleshy ridge on its back.

### ◄ RESTING PORPOISE

A Dall's porpoise displays the body features of its species. It has a stocky black body, with a large white patch on the sides and belly. Its dorsal fin and tail flukes have flashes of white as well. Unlike most porpoises, which are shy, the Dall's porpoise loves to bow-ride fast boats.

### ▼ RARE SNEEZER

Like all river dolphins, the Yangtze river dolphin, or baiji, has poor sight. Its blowhole is circular and its blow sounds like a sneeze! This dolphin is one of the rarest of all cetaceans, numbering maybe only 150 individuals.

Did you know? The harbor porpoise is rarely seen in harbors.

## ▶ FAST AND FURIOUS

Dall's porpoises are the most energetic of all porpoises. Their swimming is fast and furious. They kick up great fountains of spray as they thrust themselves through the surface of the water.

## ▶ NOISY SNORTER

The harbor porpoise seldom comes near boats. It has a noisy, snorting blow. The general body color is dark gray on the back with paler patches on the flanks. Its belly is white, and it has black flippers and lips.

Did you know? Dall's porpoises are one of the fastest marine mammals—traveling up to 35 knots.

## ▼ DOLPHIN OR PORPOISE?

Porpoises are close relatives of dolphins, but they belong to a different family with different body features. Scientists can take advantage of strandings such as this one to study these very shy creatures.

59

# Fellow Travelers

Whales are not the only aquatic mammals. Other examples include otters and seals. Seals are well adapted to life in the water, with a sleek, streamlined body and flippers. They have some fur, but it is the thick layer of fatty blubber under the skin that keeps them warm in the water. It also insulates against the cold air when seals are on land. The dugong and the manatee are also at home in the water. Often called sea cows, these creatures have a bulky seal-like body. They live in rivers and coastal waters in tropical and subtropical regions.

## ▲ BEAR AT SEA

The polar bear drifts on pack ice in the Arctic Ocean, often taking to the water to hunt seals. In addition to a thick layer of blubber, a polar bear has a thick furry coat to protect it from the Arctic climate.

## ◄ FIN-FOOTED

The Californian sea lion swims using powerful strokes of its front flippers. Its body is much more adapted to the water than an otter's, with its paddle-like flippers. Its body is partly hairy, partly smooth.

**Did you know?** Whales were probably descended from a 4-legged land mammal called a mesonychid.

## ► FURRY SWIMMER

The otter is at home on land or in water. Its four-legged, furry body is adapted for life in the water. Its legs are short, and its toes are webbed, making efficient paddles. Its fur is waterproof.

## ▲ WHALE-LIKE

The whale shark is not a whale, but the biggest fish of all—a harmless member of the shark family. The whale shark measures more than 49 ft long. It feeds on plankton, which it takes in through its gaping mouth. It sieves out the plankton from the water through a special gill structure.

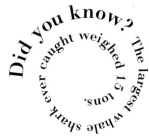

Did you know? The largest whale shark ever caught weighed 15 tons.

## ◄ SEA COW

A dugong swims in the Pacific Ocean, just off Australia. Unlike the seals, which leave the water to breed on land, dugongs spend all their time in the sea. They have no hind limbs, but a tail, similar to that of a whale. The alternative name for the creature—sea cow—is a good one because the animal feeds on sea grasses.

## ► EXCAVATOR

The walrus is a mammal of the seal family. Like the true seals, it has no external ears and it swims by means of its rear flippers. It feeds mainly on the seabed, using its whiskers to locate buried clams and its armored snout to grub them out. The walrus excavates clams by squirting a high pressure jet of water from its mouth into the clam's burrow.

# Whale Slaughter

The baleen whales and sperm whale are so big that they have no natural predators. Until a few hundred years ago, the oceans teemed with them. In the 15th and 16th centuries, whaling grew into a huge industry. Whales were killed for blubber, which could be rendered down into oils for candles and lamps. The industry expanded following the invention of an explosive harpoon gun in the 1860s, and by the 1930s nearly 50,000 whales a year were taken in Antarctica. In 1988, commercial whaling was banned.

▲ **WHALE SOAP**
The sperm whale was once a prime target for whalers. They were after the waxy spermaceti from the organ in the whale's forehead. This was used to make soap.

▶ **DEADLY STRUGGLE**
Whalers row out from a big ship to harpoon a whale in the early 1800s. It was a dangerous occupation in those days because the dying whales could easily smash the small boats to pieces.

**Did you know?** Whale blubber was made into lipstick and other sorts of make-up.

▼ **FIN WHALING**
A modern whaler finishes cutting up a fin whale. A few whales are still caught legally for scientific purposes, but their meat ends up on the table in some countries. The fin whale used to be a favorite target for whalers because of its huge size.

◄ **PILOT MASSACRE**
Every year in the Faroe Islands of the North Atlantic pods of pilot whales are killed, a traditional practice that has not been stopped. The blood of the dying whales turns the sea red.

*Did you know? Early whalers killed their prey by throwing harpoons from row boats.*

► **KILLER NET**
This striped dolphin died when it was caught in a drift net. It became entangled and was unable to rise to the surface to breathe. Tens of thousands of dolphins drown each year because of nets cast into the oceans.

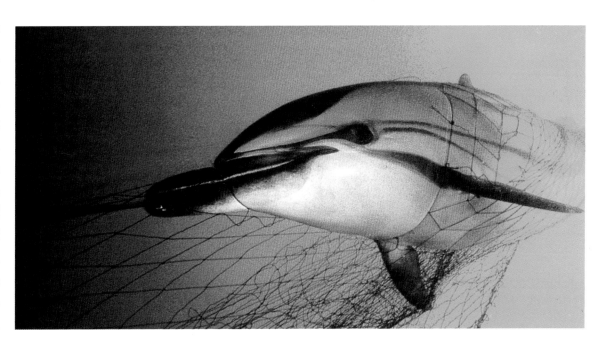

*Did you know? In the 1800s, baleen was used to make umbrellas.*

**"Whale Tale"**
Moby Dick *was written by Herman Melville in 1851. The one-legged Captain Ahab searches for a great white whale (a sperm whale) called Moby Dick. Eventually he harpoons Moby Dick, but he and all but one of his crew die.*

THE SPERMACETI WHALE

# Whale Conservation

If full-scale whaling had continued, many of the great whales would now be extinct. Even today, only a few thousand blue whales, right whales and bowhead whales remain. Because they are slow breeders, it will take a long time for numbers to recover. However the gray whale and the humpback whale appear to be recovering well. These two whales are favorites among whale-watchers because they are so approachable. Whale-watching has made people aware of what remarkable creatures whales are and why they must be protected.

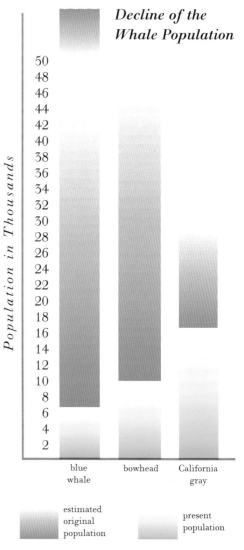

*Decline of the Whale Population*

Population in Thousands

50
48
46
44
42
40
38
36
34
32
30
28
26
24
22
20
18
16
14
12
10
8
6
4
2

blue whale    bowhead    California gray

estimated original population

present population

### ▲ GRAY GREETING

A gray whale surfaces near a boat off the Pacific coast of Mexico. It is winter, and the grays have migrated to these warmer breeding grounds from the far north. Because these animals stay close to the shore, they are easy to reach by boat.

Did you know? The first whale sanctuary was set up in 1945.

### ▲ WHALE RECOVERY

By the middle of the 20th century, the blue, bowhead and gray whales were close to extinction. Then whaling was banned. Now populations are recovering.

### ▼ HUMPBACK SPECTACULAR

A humpback whale breaches. It hurls its 30-ton bulk into the air, belly up, and will soon crash back to the surface. Out of all the behavior whale-watchers come to see, this is by far the most spectacular.

## ▶ FRIENDLY FLIPPER

One bottlenose dolphin character, called Flipper, (played by several dolphins), starred in a series of TV programs and films. These focused attention on how intelligent dolphins are.

*Did you know? You can adopt your own whale by contacting your own local whale and dolphin organization.*

## ◀ WHALE-WATCHING

A boatload of whale-watchers sees the tail flukes of a humpback whale disappear as the animal starts to dive. The boat is cruising off the New England coast where some populations of humpbacks feed during the summer months.

## ▶ PERFORMING KILLER

A killer whale leaps high out of the water at a dolphinarium, drawing applause from the huge crowd watching. In the wild, the killer whale is an adept predator, and in captivity—like all wild animals, can be unpredictable. However, many people believe it is cruel to capture and keep them penned up.

*Did you know? Some countries continue to hunt whales.*

# SHARKS

Sharks have gills with which they absorb oxygen from seawater and so do not need to surface to breathe. Some have to keep moving in order that oxygen-rich water passes over their gills, and others can actively pump water over their gills. The former must keep moving throughout their lives or they will drown, while the latter can rest on the bottom, although they are such efficient swimmers that they use more energy "resting" than when they are moving!

# What is a Shark?

There are about 400 different kinds of shark in the world. Some are as big as whales, others as small as a cigar. Whatever their size, they all eat meat. Some sharks eat tiny plants and animals called plankton. Others hunt down fish, squid, and even seals. Many sharks will also feed off the remains of another's meal or eat animal carcasses. They live at all depths, in every ocean, from tropical waters to cold polar seas. Some sharks can survive in the fresh water of rivers and lakes. Like other fish, sharks take oxygen from the water as it passes over their gills. Although some sharks like to live alone, others survive as part of a group.

▼ CLASSIC SHARK

This blue shark (*Prionace glauca*) is how most people imagine sharks. However, there are many different families of sharks in the seas and oceans and with a variety of body shapes.

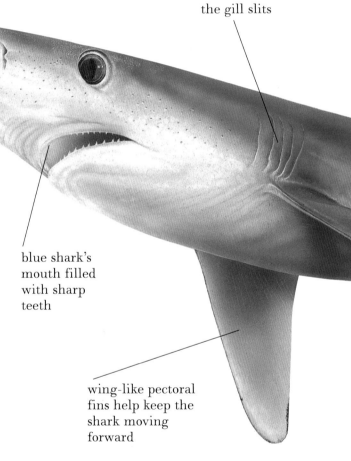

no cover over the gill slits

blue shark's mouth filled with sharp teeth

wing-like pectoral fins help keep the shark moving forward

◄ WHITE DEATH

The great white shark (*Carcharodon carcharias*) is the largest hunting fish in the sea. It has an exaggerated reputation as a killer, partly because a killer shark appears in the film, *Jaws*. In reality great white sharks do often eat large prey, but they attack people only occasionally, in cases of mistaken identity.

**▶ SHARK SCHOOL**
Some sharks live alone, others live in schools (groups). Every day schools of female scalloped hammerhead sharks (*Sphyra lewini*) like these gather off the Mexican coast. At night, the sharks separate and hunt alone.

triangular dorsal (back) fin for stability

body packed with muscles for strength

**▲ GENTLE GIANT**
Although the basking shark (*Cetorhinus maximus*) is the second largest fish after the whale shark, it is not a hunter. It funnels water through its huge mouth, using gill rakers (giant combs) to filter out the tiny plankton that it eats.

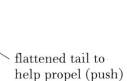

flattened tail to help propel (push) through water

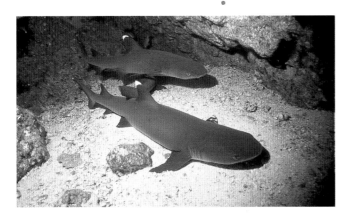

**▲ REEF HUNTERS**
Whitetip reef sharks (*Triaenodon obesus*) are one of the smaller species (kinds) of shark. They rarely grow over 6 ft long and hunt along tropical coral reefs at night.

***Maya Origins***
*This monkey head from Central America has been decorated with shark teeth. It is thought that the word shark comes from the Maya people of Central America. It may be based on the Maya word* xoc, *(fury). The Maya symbol (word picture) for* xoc *is a shark-like creature.*

69

# Shapes and Sizes

Many hunting sharks have long, rounded shapes, like the slim blue shark and the bulkier bull shark. Angel sharks have a flattened shape suited to hiding on the sea floor, while eel-like frilled sharks swim in the deep sea. Horn sharks have spines on their back, and megamouths (big mouths) have big, blubbery lips! As their names suggest, hammerhead sharks have hammer-shaped heads, and sawsharks have elongated, saw-like snouts. Giant sharks, such as the whale shark, are as long as a school bus, and there are midget sharks, such as the Colombian lantern shark, that you could hold in the palm of your hand! Whatever the kind of shark, they are all perfectly adapted for the waters in which they live.

## ▲ GROTESQUE SHARK

The goblin shark (*Mitsukurina owstoni*) has an unusual, horn-shaped snout. This shark seems to have also lived in the dinosaur age. A fossil of a similar shark has been found in rocks that were created about 150 million years ago. Today, the goblin shark lives in very deep waters found off continental shelves.

## ▶ DEEP SEA NIPPER

The pygmy shark is one of the smallest sharks in the world. When fully grown, it is no more than 8 in. long, making it smaller than a whale shark embryo (baby). It roams the gloomy waters of the Caribbean Sea, hunting in packs.

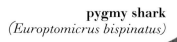

**pygmy shark**
(*Europtomicrus bispinatus*)

## ▲ STRANGE HEAD

The amazing heads of the hammerhead, bonnethead and winghead sharks are shaped like the letter T. These sharks use their hammers to detect prey and to help when swimming.

zebra bullhead shark
(*Heterodontus zebra*)

Did you know? The largest shark ever measured was 37.95 ft long.

## ▲ ROCK DISGUISE

Unlike many sharks, the spotted wobbegong shark (*Orectolobus maculatus*) has a flattened shape. It is a carpet shark (a family of camouflaged sharks that lie on the seabed), and disguises itself as part of the coral reef. The tassels (barbels) under its mouth look like seaweed.

## ▲ SAFETY SPINES

A striped pattern helps the colorful zebra bullhead shark to camouflage itself (blend in) among corals and seaweed. For further protection, at the front of each dorsal fin is a sharp spine. If swallowed, the shark's spines will stick into the throat of any attacker, forcing it eventually to spit out its prickly meal.

## ► UNDERWATER TIGER

A young tiger shark has pale stripes along its body, which fade as it grows older. The powerful tiger shark (*Galeocerdo cuvier*) has a long, rounded shape, typical of hunting sharks. Some can rival great whites in size.

## ◄ BIG GULP

The whale shark (*Rhincodon typus*) is aptly named. Bigger than any other shark, it is closer in size to the giant whales. It is the largest fish in the sea, can grow to 40–50 ft in length and weigh up to 3 tons. With its giant mouth and large gill slits, the whale shark, like the basking shark, is a filter feeder.

# Light and Strong

Although most fish are bony, the skeleton of a shark is made up almost entirely of cartilage, which is also found in the human nose. It is lighter and more elastic than bone, and it is this that makes the shark skeleton very flexible. This cartilage structure is strong enough to support a shark's huge muscles, and flexible enough to allow it to move with ease. Because sharks' skeletal cartilage and soft body parts decay (rot) so quickly after they die, it is unusual to find complete shark fossils (preserved bodies) in ancient rocks. Only the hard teeth and spines are fossilized.

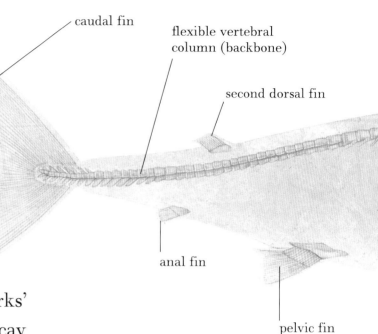

caudal fin

flexible vertebral column (backbone)

second dorsal fin

anal fin

pelvic fin

### ▼ PROTRUDING JAWS
A shark's jaws are attached to the skull by flexible ligaments. These allow some sharks to thrust their jaws forward when taking a bite.

teeth in upper jaw slice like a knife

### ▲ DARK TRIANGLE
Like the keel of a yacht, a shark's stiff dorsal fin helps it to balance in the water and stops it from slipping sideways. Most sharks have two dorsal fins, one at the front and one at the back.

## ▶ AIRPLANE FINS

A shark's pectoral fins, one on each side, act like the wings of an airplane. As water passes over them, the fins give lift.

dorsal fin

gill arches support shark's gills

compact skull protects brain and nasal capsules.

pectoral fin

## ◀ SHARK SKELETON

The skeleton of a great white shark. It is tough, flexible and typical of that found in most sharks, providing support and protection for the entire body. The great white's muscles are attached to a long backbone; the gills are supported by gill arches and a box-like skull protects the brain.

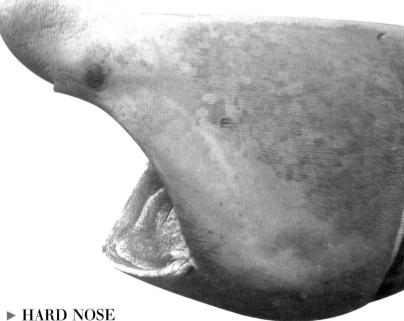

## ▲ CARTILAGE SOUP

These fins have been cut from sharks and are drying in the sun. The cartilage in a shark's fin helps to make it stiff. When boiled in water it makes a gluey substance that is used in the Far East to make shark's fin soup.

## ▶ HARD NOSE

The shark pictured above is an adult basking shark. At birth, this shark has a strange, hooked nose, like that of an elephant. When the basking shark starts to grow, the cartilage in its snout gradually straightens.

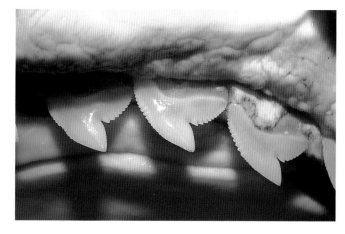

▲ **SHARK SAW MASSACRE**
The teeth of a tiger shark are shaped like the letter L. They can saw through skin, muscle and bone, and can even crack open the hard shell of a sea turtle. A tiger shark eats its prey by biting hard and shaking its head from side to side, slicing into its food like a chain saw.

▼ **AWESOME JAWS**
When it is about to grab its prey, a sandtiger shark opens and extends its awesome jaws. The rows of spiky teeth inside are perfect for grabbing and holding slippery fish and squid. Once caught, the prey is swallowed whole.

**sandtiger shark**
(*Eugomphodus taurus*)

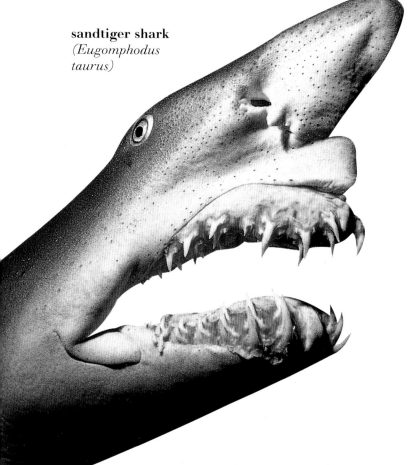

# Tough Teeth

A shark species can be identified by the shape of its teeth alone. Each species has its own distinctive shape, designed for the type of food it eats. Some have sharp, spiky teeth that can hold on to slippery fish and squid. Others have broad, grinding teeth that can crack open shellfish. The teeth of some species of shark change as they get older and hunt different prey. Although sharks lose their teeth regularly, the teeth are always replaced. Behind each row of teeth lie more rows. If a front tooth is dislodged, an extra tooth simply moves forward to take its place!

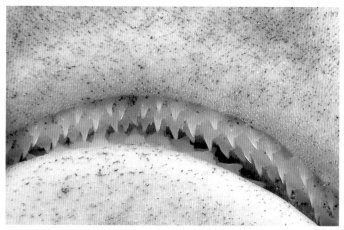

▲ **NEEDLE POINT**
This 6-ft-long leopard shark (*Triakis semifasciata*) has rows of small, needle-sharp, teeth. Although it is thought to be harmless, in 1955 a leopard shark sunk its tiny teeth into a skin diver in Trinidad Bay, California. This was an unprovoked attack, and the diver escaped.

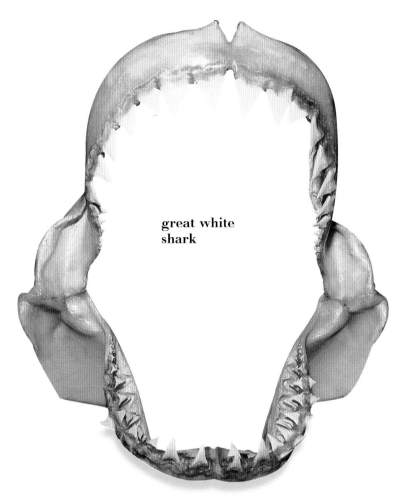

great white shark

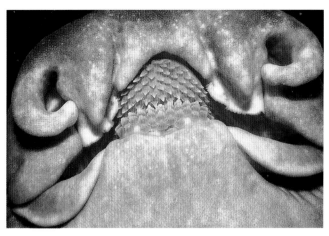

## ▲ DUAL SETS OF TEETH

The Port Jackson shark (*Heterodontus portusjacksoni*) has small, sharp teeth for catching small fish and broad, crushing teeth that can crack open shellfish.

## ▼ BIG TEETH

The cookie-cutter is a small shark, reaching only 20 in. long. However, for its body size, it has the biggest teeth of any shark known. It uses them to cut round chunks out of its prey, which includes dolphins, whales and large fish.

## ▲ JAWS

The awesome jaws of a great white shark are filled with two types of teeth. The upper jaw is lined with large, triangular teeth that can slice through flesh. The lower jaw contains long, pointed teeth that are used to hold and slice prey.

### Shark Man
*Ceremonial carvings such as this one were used in ritual dances performed in the South Pacific Solomon Islands. From one dance master to another, these traditional dances were passed down through many generations. They told of myths in which sharks turned into men, and men turned back into sharks again.*

cookie-cutter shark (*Isistius brasiliensis*)

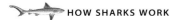 

# Shark Bodies

Sharks are incredible machines, packed with muscle. Some sharks, such as the great white and mako, can even keep their muscles, gut, brain, and eyes warmer than the temperature of the seawater around them. They do this with special blood vessels, which work like a radiator to collect the heat in the blood and send it back into the body. These make muscles more efficient, allowing the sharks to swim faster. They also help these sharks to hunt in seas of different temperatures. Sharks have a huge, oil-filled liver that helps to keep them afloat. However, like an airplane, they must also move forward in order to stay up. Open ocean sharks must swim all the time, not only to stop them from sinking, but also to breathe. Some sharks can take a rest on the seabed by pumping water over their gills to breathe.

**▲ GILL BREATHERS**
Like this sixgill shark (*Hexanchus griseus*), most sharks breathe by taking oxygen-rich water into their mouths. The oxygen passes into the blood and the water exits the gill slits.

**▲ OCEAN RACER**
The shortfin mako shark (*Isurus oxyrinchus*) is the fastest shark in the sea. Using special, warm muscles, it can travel at speeds of 20–30 mph and catch fast-swimming swordfish.

**◀ SUSPENDED ANIMATION**
The sandtiger shark (*Eugomphodus taurus*) and a few others can hold air in their stomachs. The air acts like a life jacket, helping the shark to hover in the water. Sandtiger sharks stay afloat without moving, lurking among rocks and caves.

► **KEEP MOVING**

Like many hunting sharks, the gray reef shark (*Carcharinhus amblyrynchos*) cannot breathe unless it moves forward. The forward motion passes oxygen into its gills. If it stops moving, the shark will drown.

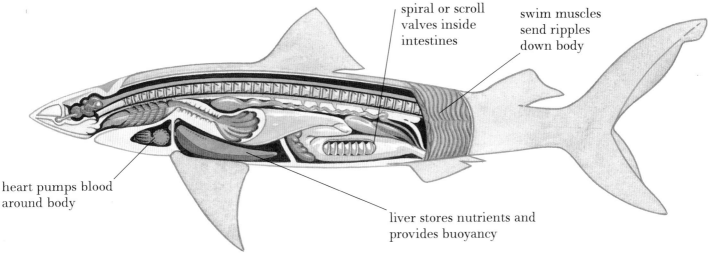

spiral or scroll valves inside intestines

swim muscles send ripples down body

heart pumps blood around body

liver stores nutrients and provides buoyancy

▲ **INSIDE A SHARK**

If you could look inside a shark, you would find thick muscles, an enormous liver, an intestine with a special, spiral valve, and a complicated system of blood vessels that supply the shark's gills.

**Did you know?** Mako sharks have been seen to leap 20 ft clear of the water.

◄ **ABLE TO REST**

The tawny nurse shark (*Nebrius ferrugineus*) pumps water over its gills by lifting the floor of its mouth. This allows it to rest on the seabed, yet still breathe. Whitetip reef sharks, lemon sharks, catsharks and nursehounds also do this.

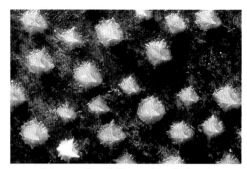
skin teeth of Greenland shark

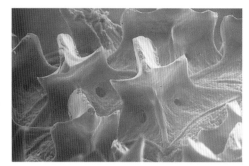
skin teeth of spiny dogfish

skin teeth of dusky shark

## ▲ SKIN TEETH

A shark's skin is covered with tiny skin teeth called dermal denticles. These teeth help to speed the shark through the water by controlling the flow of water over its body.

## ▶ STREAMLINED SHARK

The upper part of the gray reef shark's tail is slightly larger than the lower. Because of this, the tail's downward movement is so powerful that it balances the lift from the pectoral wings. Scientists believe that this helps the shark to move evenly through the water.

# Wings in Water

A shark has two pairs of fins (pectoral and pelvic) that work like an airplane's wings, lifting the shark as it moves forward. Its dorsal fins and anal fin stop it from rolling sideways, like the tail fin of an aircraft. A shark moves forward in an S shape by rippling a series of waves down its entire body. These waves increase in size as they reach the shark's tail, helping it to propel the body forward. The shape of the tail can vary from shark to shark, depending on the area of water it inhabits. Sharks that live at the bottom of the sea, such as the nurse shark, tend to have large, flat tails. Sharks that swim in open oceans, such as the tiger shark, usually have slimmer, more curved tails. Both types have a larger upper part to their tail. Sharks that stalk and dash to catch their prey, such as the great white and mako shark, have crescent-shaped tails with top and bottom parts the same size.

## ▲ SEABED SWIMMERS

Hammerhead sharks have unusually small pectoral fins, which allow them to swim and feed close to the seabed. The wings of the hammer-shaped head give the shark extra lift in the water and allow it to turn very tightly. Hammerhead sharks are very adaptable and skillful hunters.

## ▲ DEEP SEA GIANT

The megamouth shark (*Megachasma pelagios*) was only discovered in 1976. It lives in deep water and swims very slowly. Megamouth does not chase anything. It eats deep-sea shrimps filtered through its gills.

## ▲ OCEAN TRAVELER

The blue shark (*Prionace glauca*) has long pectoral fins that help it to sail through the sea like a glider plane, making long journeys easy. It swims to the surface, then glides effortlessly to the depths before swimming back to the surface again.

## ▲ OCEAN CRUISER

The oceanic whitetip shark (*Carcharhinus longimanus*) swims in the open oceans and is often present at the scene of sea disasters. It is a very distinctive shark, and can be easily recognized by its dorsal and pectoral fins, which are shaped like rounded garden spades.

# Brain and Senses

A shark's brain is small for its size, but its senses are highly developed. Sharks see well, and see in color. They can also recognize shapes. Just as amazing are a different range of senses that allow sharks to pick up sounds and vibrations from miles around. They can detect changes in the ocean currents, recognize smells and follow the trail of an odor right back to its source. Some species have shiny plates at the backs of their eyes that collect light to help them see as they dive into deep, dark water. They also have dark membranes that they draw across the shiny plates to keep from being dazzled by the light when they return to the surface. Sharks even have special nerves in their noses that can detect minute electrical fields, such as those produced by the muscles of their prey.

## ▲ ELECTRICAL SENSE

Like all sharks, sandtiger sharks have tiny pits in their snouts, known as the ampullae of Lorenzini. Inside these pits are special nerves. These help the shark to find food by detecting minute electrical fields in the muscles of its prey.

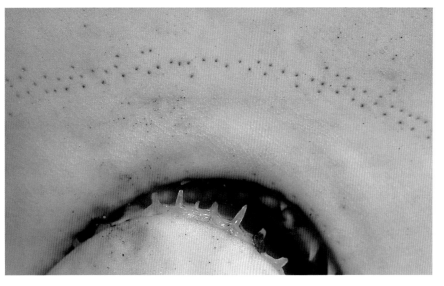

## ◀ PREY DETECTOR

In a hammerhead shark the special pits that can sense electrical fields in its prey are spread across the hammer of the shark's head, helping it to scan for prey across a wide area. The hammerhead searches for food by sweeping its head from side to side, as if it was using a metal detector. It can find any prey buried in the sand below.

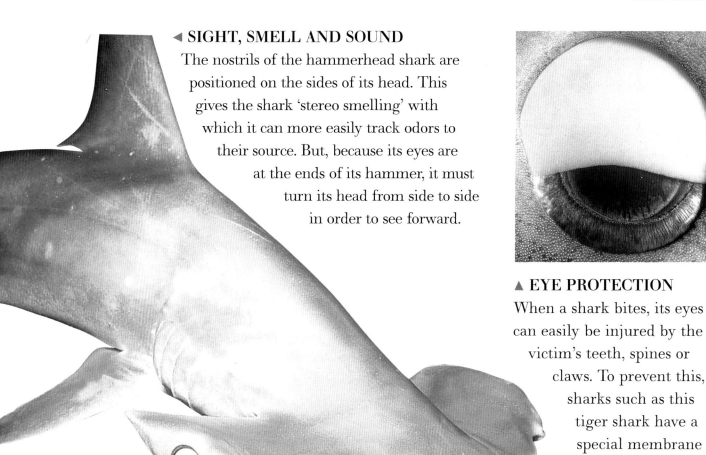

## ◄ SIGHT, SMELL AND SOUND

The nostrils of the hammerhead shark are positioned on the sides of its head. This gives the shark 'stereo smelling' with which it can more easily track odors to their source. But, because its eyes are at the ends of its hammer, it must turn its head from side to side in order to see forward.

scalloped
hammerhead shark
(*Sphyrna lewini*)

## ▲ EYE PROTECTION

When a shark bites, its eyes can easily be injured by the victim's teeth, spines or claws. To prevent this, sharks such as this tiger shark have a special membrane (sheath) that slides down across the eye during the attack.

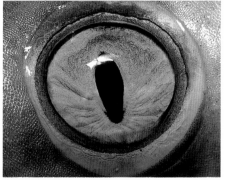

eye of blacktip reef shark
(*Carcharhinus melanopterus*)

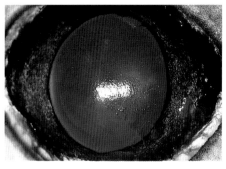

eye of bluntnose sixgill shark
(*Hexanchus griseus*)

## ◄ DEEP AND SHALLOW

The blacktip reef shark has a small eye with a narrow, vertical slit. This type of eye is often found in shallow-water sharks. Sharks that swim in deeper waters, such as the sixgill shark, tend to have large, round pupils.

Did you know? Sharks find their way through mazes as fast as rabbits.

*Shark Callers*
*On the islands of the southwest Pacific, sharks are the islanders' gods. To test their manhood, young shark callers attract sharks by shaking a coconut rattle under the water. Sensing the vibrations, a shark will swim close to the canoe. It is then wrestled into the boat, and its meat divided among the villagers as a gift from the gods.*

81

# Focus on the Blue

The blue shark is an open ocean hunter. Continually looking for food, it can pick up the sounds and vibrations of a struggling fish from a half mile away. From a quarter of a mile, it can smell blood and other body fluids in the water. As it gets closer, the shark can sense changes in the water that help it locate moving prey. Finally, vision takes over. First, only movements are seen, but then the prey itself. As the blue shark closes in for the kill, it pulls down its eye protectors and swims blind. Its electrical sensors then lead it to its prey.

2 Smells, sounds, vibrations, and water movements attract the blue shark. The movements made by a school of jack mackerel will initially lead the shark to them. It then uses its sight to find an easy target.

1 When hunting, the blue shark uses all its senses to constantly search the ocean ahead for prey. It will also watch the behavior of other blue sharks in the water, sometimes joining them to hunt in packs.

# Shark Hunt

3 Sharp eyesight, quick reactions and an ability to speed through the water all help the blue shark to chase its chosen target. In an attempt to escape, this group of mackerel fish will dart all over the place, then crowd close together to confuse the pursuing shark.

4 As the blue shark closes in to grab its target, a protective membrane covers each eye. At this stage the shark is swimming blind and relies on the electrical sensors in its snout to guide it to its prey. These home in on the electrical field made by the fish's muscles, leading the shark for the last few inches.

5 As the shark bites, it extends its jaws and impales its prey on the teeth of the lower jaw. Next, the upper jaw teeth come into action, clamping down on the fish. The shark then removes its lower jaw teeth from the prey, and pushes them forward to pull the fish back into its mouth. The prey is then swallowed by the shark.

# Feeding

Sharks catch a variety of foods, eating whatever they can find in their area. Most sharks eat bony fish and squid, but they can be cannibalistic (eat each other). They often feed on other smaller sharks, sometimes even on their own species. Some sharks prefer particular kinds of food. Hammerheads like sting rays, while tiger sharks will crunch a sea turtle's shell for the meat inside. Shortfin mako sharks hunt bluefish and swordfish. Great white sharks eat fish, but as they get older will also hunt seals and sea lions. Sharks will scavenge (feed on dead animals) whenever they can. The bodies of dead whales are food for many sharks that swim in open waters, including tigers, blues and oceanic whitetips.

▲ **FEEDING FRENZY**
Large quantities of food will excite gray reef sharks, sending them into a feeding frenzy. When divers hand out food, the sharks will circle with interest, until one darts forward for the first bite. Other sharks quickly follow, grabbing at the food until they seem out of control.

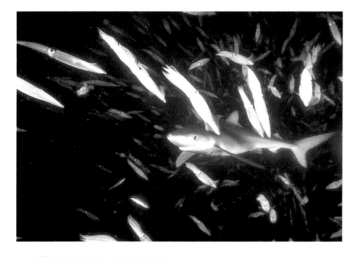

▲ **FOREVER EATING**
A large school of mating squid will send blue sharks into a frenzy. The sharks feed until full, then empty their stomachs to start again!

▲ **FISH BALL**
A group of sharks will often herd schools of fish into a tight ball. The sharks will then pick off fish from the outside of the ball, one by one.

### ▶ BITE A BROTHER

Sharks do not take care of their relatives! Big sharks will often eat smaller sharks, and sharks that swim side by side in the same school will often take a nip out of each other. The remains caught on a fishing line of this blacktip shark show that it has been eaten by a large bull shark.

*Did you know? The great white shark sometimes eats crabs and lobsters.*

### ◀ OCEAN TRASH CAN

Tiger sharks are well known as the sharks that eat more than just living things such as fish, other sharks or dead animals floating in the sea. Tiger sharks have been known to eat coal, rubber tires and clothes. They are found all over the world and grow to a length of 16½ ft. Not surprisingly, tiger sharks have been known to try eating humans.

### ▼ BITE-SIZE CHUNKS

The cookie-cutter shark feeds by cutting chunks out of whales and dolphins, such as this spinner dolphin. The shark uses its mouth like a clamp, attaching itself to its victim. It then bites with its razor-sharp teeth and swivels to twist off a circle of flesh.

**spinner dolphin**
*(Stenella longirostris)*

### ▲ OPPORTUNISTS

Sharks will often follow fishing boats, looking for a free meal. This silvertip shark is eating pieces of tuna that have been thrown overboard.

85

# Focus on

**1** Huge groups of albatrosses nest on the ground close to the shore of Hawaiian islands, including the island of Laysan. The birds in each group breed, nest, and hatch their babies at the same time. When it is time, the young birds all take their first flight within days of each other.

Sharks can be found wherever there is food in or near the sea. Tiger sharks are rarely seen around some Hawaiian islands in the Pacific Ocean until the islands' young seabirds start to fly. Then the sharks arrive. Any birds that fall into the sea are quickly eaten. The waters are too shallow for the sharks to attack from behind and below as most sharks do. Instead, the sharks leap out of the water, then drag the birds underwater to drown and eat them. Sharks arrive for their island feast at the same time each year. How they remember to do so has yet to be explained.

**2** When ready to fly, a baby bird practices by flapping its wings in the face of the islands' fierce winds. Eventually, the baby must make its first real flight over the ocean. When it does so, the tiger sharks are waiting in the water below.

**3** Tiger sharks patrol the clear, shallow waters close to the albatross nests. Their dark shapes can be seen clearly against the sandy sea floor. Every now and again, a tiger shark's triangular dorsal fin and the tip of its tail can be seen breaking the water's surface.

# Tiger Sharks

4 Any baby bird that dips into the sea is prey for the waiting tiger shark. At first, the shark tries its usual attack, from below and behind. However, in the shallow waters the shark cannot make a full attack. Rather than hitting its prey at full force, the shark just pushes the bird away on the wave made by its snout.

5 After failing to catch a meal, the shark soon realizes its mistake and tries another approach. Its next style of attack is to shoot across the surface of the water, slamming into its target with its mouth wide open. This technique seems to be more successful, and the shark usually catches the bird.

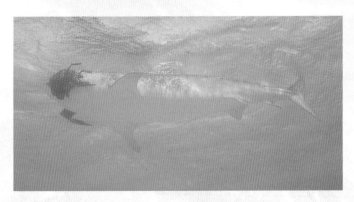

6 The shark then attempts to drag the bird below the surface, to drown it. If a bird is pushed ahead on the shark's bow wave, it will bravely peck at its attacker's broad snout and, sometimes, may even escape. Some birds also manage to wriggle free as the shark grapples with them underwater.

7 Many albatross babies do not manage to escape a shark attack. They are grabbed by the sharks and drowned. Inside the tiger shark's jaws are rows of sharp teeth that can slice into a bird's body like a saw. Sometimes the tiger shark tears off the bird's wings and set them aside to eat the body whole.

# Filter Feeders

Some of the biggest fish in the sea eat some of the smallest living things there. Giant species, like the whale shark and basking shark, use their gill rakers to comb plankton (tiny animals and plants) from the water. In the same way as hunting sharks, they use their sharp senses to track down huge areas of food. Whale sharks are often seen near coral reefs, where, at certain times of the year, large amounts of animal plankton can be found. Basking sharks often swim in the area between ocean currents, feeding on plankton that gather on the boundary. Whale and basking sharks swim in the upper layers of the sea. The giant megamouth shark lives deeper down, sieving out the shrimps that live in the middle layers of the ocean.

### ▲ FOOD CHAIN
Eggs and sperm released on the same night by the corals of the Ningaloo Reef in Australia are eaten by the larvae (young) of crabs and lobsters. The larvae are eaten by fish and krill. The fish and krill in turn become food for the hungry whale sharks that swim off the coral reefs.

### ◄ WHALE OF A FEAST
Exactly two weeks after the coral has spawned at Ningaloo, the whale sharks appear. By this time, each creature, from the smallest larvae to the reef's fish and krill, will have fed upon the coral's rich food. Each night, the whale sharks swim with their huge mouths wide open, scooping up food that they sieve from the sea's surface.

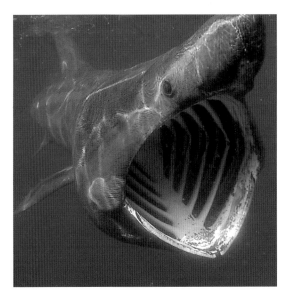

## ▲ BIG GULP

The basking shark swims slowly through the sea, funneling food-filled water into its huge mouth. In one hour, it can filter 7,000 quarts of seawater! When enough food has been trapped, the shark closes its mouth and swallows with one gulp.

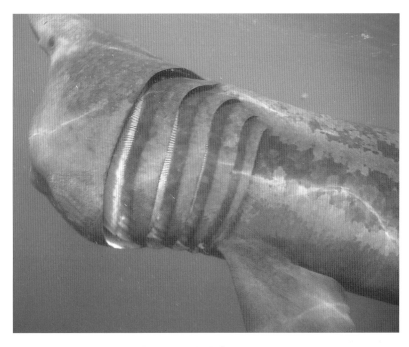

## ▲ COLD WATER SKIMMERS

The basking shark has gill slits that almost encircle its gigantic body. These are used to filter food, such as shellfish larvae and fish eggs, from the water. The shark passes water through its gill chamber, where enormous gill rakers comb the food from the water.

## ▲ BIG MOUTH

Patrolling the middle waters of the deep, the megamouth shark scoops up tiny shrimps as they cross its path. Since this shark's discovery in 1976, another 13 examples have been discovered and some of these have been examined by scientists.

## ▲ PLANKTON

Plankton is made up of tiny plants and animals that float together in huge clouds on and just below the sea's surface. Both animal and plant plankton are eaten by the basking shark.

# Stay in Line

No shark is alone for long. Sooner or later, one shark will come across another, including those of its own kind. In order to reduce the risk of fights and injury, sharks talk to each other, not with sound, but with body language. Sharks have a clear pecking order. The bigger the shark, the more important it is. Not surprisingly, small sharks tend to keep out of the way of larger ones. Many species use a sign that tells others to keep their distance. They arch their back, point their pectoral fins down and swim stiffly. If this doesn't work, the offending shark will be put in its place with a swift bite to the sides or head. Bite marks along its gill slits can be a sign that a shark has stepped out of line and been told firmly to watch out.

▲ **GREAT WHITE CHUMS**
Great white sharks were once thought to travel alone, but it is now known that some journey in pairs or small groups. Some sharks that have been identified by scientists will appear repeatedly at favorite sites, such as California's Farallon Islands, 24 mi. off the coast of San Francisco. There they lie in wait for seals.

*Did you know? Some great whites return to the same spot every year.*

◄ **BED FELLOWS**
Sharks, like these whitetip reef sharks, will snooze alongside each other on the seabed. They search for a safe place to rest below overhanging rocks and coral, where, as fights rarely break out, they seem to tolerate each other. The sharks remain here until dusk, when they separate to hunt.

### ◀ PECKING ORDER

This gray reef shark has swum too close to another, larger shark and has been bitten on its gill slits as a punishment. The marks on its skin show that its attacker raked the teeth of its lower jaw across the sensitive skin of the gray reef's gill slits. A shark's injuries heal rapidly, so this unfortunate victim will recover quickly from its wounds.

### ▶ REEF SHARK GANGS

Sharks have their own personal space. As they patrol the edge of a reef, schools of blacktip reef sharks will tell others that they are too close by moving their jaw or opening their mouth. During feeding, order sometimes breaks down, and a shark might be injured in the frenzy.

### ◀ SHARK SCHOOL

Every day schools of scalloped hammerhead sharks gather close to underwater mountains in the Pacific Ocean. They do not feed, even though they come across schools of fish that would normally be food. Instead, they swim repeatedly up and down, as though taking a rest.

# FOCUS ON

By day, scalloped hammerhead sharks swim in large schools around underwater volcanoes in the Pacific, the Gulf of California off Mexico, and off the Coco and Galapagos islands. This species of shark cannot stop swimming or it will drown. Schools are a safe resting place for them. Even sharks have enemies, such as other sharks and killer whales, so there is safety in numbers. In schools, scalloped hammerheads can also find a mate. At night, they separate to hunt. They swim to favorite feeding sites, using their electric sensors to follow magnetic highways made by lava on the seabed.

**BAD-TEMPERED SHARKS**
The larger a female hammerhead becomes, the less likely she is to get along with her neighbors! Older and larger hammerhead sharks like more space than smaller, younger sharks. In hammerhead schools, the relationship between sharks seems to be controlled by constant displays of threat and small fights.

**FEMALES ONLY**
The sharks in this huge school of hammerheads are mainly females. Larger sharks swim in the center, and smaller sharks on the outside. Large sharks dominate the group, choosing the best positions in which to swim. Not only is the middle safer, but it is also the place where male sharks look for a mate.

# Hammerheads

## READY FOR A SCRUB

At some gathering sites, such as Cocos Island in the eastern Pacific, sharks drop out of the school and swoop down to cleaning stations close to the reef. From the reef, butterfly fish dart out to eat the dead skin and irritating parasites that cling to the outside of the shark's body.

## BODY LANGUAGE

Larger sharks within a school perform strange movements and dances to keep smaller sharks in their place. At the end of the movement, a large shark may nip a smaller one on the back of the head!

## STRANGE HEAD

The scalloped hammerhead is so named because of the groove at the front of its head, which gives it a scalloped (scooped out) appearance. The black tips on the underside of its pectoral fins are another way of identifying this particular shark.

# Courtship and Mating

Male sharks find female sharks by their smell. The female gives off odors that drift in the currents of the sea, attracting every male shark within smelling distance. The males follow her closely, until one grabs hold of a pectoral fin with his mouth and hangs on tightly in preparation for mating. Fortunately, the female has thickened skin on her pectoral fins, which prevents her from being hurt. The male has a pair of claspers (sex organs), one of which he places inside the female's sexual opening. During mating, the male shark shakes occasionally, to make sure that the female accepts his presence. Once he is sure of this, the male will complete his mating with her.

▲ **ENGAGEMENT IN THE SHALLOWS**
A group of male whitetip sharks will be stimulated by the smell of a female ready to mate. Following her in the shallow waters of a coral reef, the males compete for the female. Eventually, one will win possession by grabbing hold of one of her pectoral fins.

◀ **HANGING AROUND**
Sandtiger sharks hover in the water at special meeting places, waiting for members of the opposite sex. At these sites, lots of shark teeth are found on the sea floor. It is believed that they fall out during the rough and tumble of courtship and mating.

## ◀ THREE IS A CROWD
Male sharks are usually smaller than females of the same age. Here two males have each seized a female's pectoral fin, but only one male will be able to mate with her.

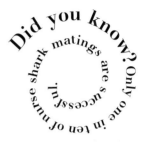
Did you know? Only one in ten of nurse shark matings are successful.

## ▶ NURSE SHARK NUPTIALS
Nurse sharks (*Ginglymostoma cirratum*) travel to traditional mating sites. The male nurse shark grips the female's pectoral fin and arches his body alongside hers. He will then insert his right or left clasper, depending on which pectoral fin he has seized.

## ▲ MALE SEX ORGANS
The claspers (sex organs) of male sharks are pelvic fins that have been adapted for mating. Similar to the penises of mammals, they are used to transfer sperm from the male into the female.

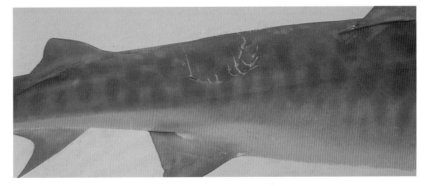

## ▲ MATING SCARS
The courtship and mating of sharks can be a rough affair. Female sharks, like this tiger shark, can be scarred with bite marks made by her mate. However, females have thicker skin than males, which prevents serious damage.

# Inside and Outside

▲ EGG WITH A TWIST
The horn shark (*Heterodontus francisci*) egg case has a spiral-shaped ridge. The mother shark uses her mouth like a screwdriver to twist the case around into the gaps in rocks.

Sharks bring their young into the world in two ways. Most sharks grow their eggs inside the mother's body, and give birth to breathing young called pups. Others lay eggs in which the pup grows outside of the mother's body. Catsharks and nursehound sharks grow their young in cases called mermaid's purses, which they lay outside their bodies. These can sometimes be found washed up on beaches after a storm. Each mating season, catsharks lay up to 20 mermaid's purses. Inside each is one pup. When the case has been laid in the sea, the mother shark does not guard or take care of it in any way. Instead, she relies on the tough, leathery case to protect the pup inside.

▲ TIME TO LEAVE
When it is ready to leave its egg, the baby horn shark uses special scales on its snout and pectoral fins to cut its way out of the tough egg case. On its dorsal fins are tough spines that protect it from the moment it emerges.

*Mermaid's Purses*
*The mermaid is a mythical undersea creature with a woman's body and a fish's tail. In legends, the mermaid lured men to their death with beautiful songs. Catshark and skate cases that are washed up on beaches look like pouches, and are often called mermaid's purses.*

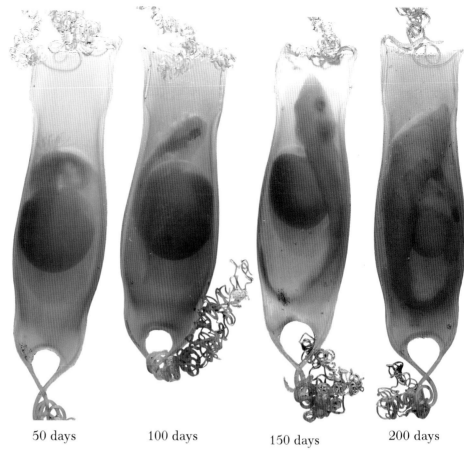

50 days      100 days      150 days      200 days

## ▲ IN THE SAC

In the earliest stages of development, the catshark pup is tiny. It is attached to a huge, yellow yolk sac from which it takes its food. Inside the egg case, the growing catshark pup makes swimming movements, which keeps the egg fluids and supply of oxygen fresh. After nine months, the pup emerges, with diagonal stripes that eventually turn into spots as it grows.

## ► SWELL SHARK

The length of time it takes the swell shark (*Cephaloscyllium ventriosum*) pup to grow depends on the temperature of the sea water around it. If warm, it can take just seven months. If cold, it might take ten months. As it emerges, it uses special skin teeth to tear its capsule open.

# Into the World

Most sharks give birth to fully formed, breathing pups. However, pups grow in many different ways. Baby nurse and whale sharks start their life in small capsules. The pups then hatch from the capsules inside their mother's body, where they continue to grow before being born. Other shark pups, like blue sharks, also grow inside their mothers, in a womb. A sandtiger shark might have just two pups, but a blue shark can grow up to 135 at one time. The length of time it takes a pup to grow also varies. Nurse sharks take just five months, but frilled sharks take two years. Some pups feed on unfertilized eggs inside the womb. Baby sandtiger sharks exhibit even more extreme behavior—they eat each other.

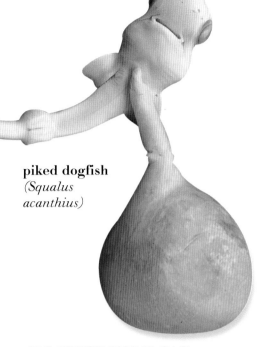

piked dogfish
(*Squalus acanthius*)

## ▲ DOGFISH YOLK SAC

Up to 12 piked dogfish pups can grow inside one mother. At first, all the pups are enclosed in one capsule that breaks after six months. Each pup then feeds off its own yolk sac until it is born three months later.

## ▶ RESTING

When birth is near, a pregnant whitetip reef shark will rest in a protective area. This pregnant shark is resting on rocks near Cocos Island in the Pacific. Inside her womb, she may develop up to five pups. Each will be fed by a placenta attached to the womb wall.

The pups are born after five months.

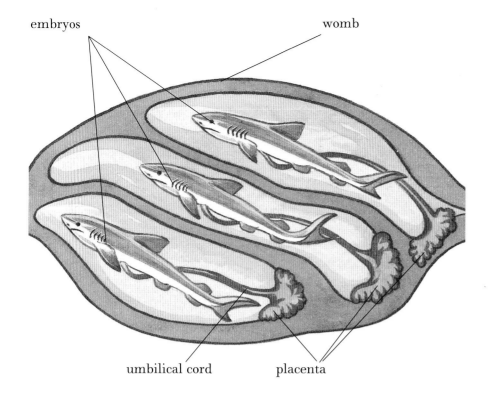

embryos womb

umbilical cord placenta

## ▲ WOMB MATES

In some species of shark, such as the whaler shark, embryos develop inside the pregnant female as they do in mammals. At first, each embryo has its own supply of food in a yolk sac, but when this is used up its sac turns into a placenta that attaches itself to the wall of the womb. Nutrients and oxygen pass directly from the mother across the placenta and along the umbilical cord to its own body. Waste products go the other way.

## ▲ BIG BELLIES

Some baby sharks will eat unfertilized eggs in their mothers' wombs. They eat so much so fast their stomachs become swollen. These baby shortfin mako sharks, caught off the coast of South Africa, have gorged on unfertilized eggs, filling their tiny stomachs.

## ◄ STRIPED SHARK

Safe inside its mother, this baby tiger shark will have fed on both the nutrients from its yolk sac, and on a fluid produced by the wall of the womb. The pattern of blotches on the newborn baby's skin will form stripes, which will gradually fade as it gets older.

# Focus on Lemon

A year after mating, pregnant lemon sharks arrive at Bimini Island in the Atlantic Ocean. Here, they give birth to their pups in the island's shallow lagoon where males do not enter. An adult male is quite likely to eat a smaller shark, even one of its own kind. In many species of shark, pregnant female sharks leave the males and swim to safer nursery areas to give birth. Some scientists even believe that females lose their appetite at pupping time, to avoid eating their own young. After birth, however, the lemon shark pups live on their own.

1 By pumping sea water over her gills, a pregnant lemon shark (*Negaprion brevirostris*) can breathe and rest on the seabed at Bimini Island. She gives birth on the sandy lagoon floor to the pups that have developed inside her for a year.

2 Baby lemon sharks are born tail first. There might be 5–17 pups in a mother's litter (family). Each pup is about 24 in. long. After her litter is born, a female lemon shark will not be able to mate again right away. Instead, she will rest for a year.

# Shark Birth

3 A female lemon shark can give birth to her pups as she swims slowly through the shallows. The pups are still attached to the umbilical cord when born, but a sharp tug soon releases them. The small remora fish that follow the shark everywhere will feast on the afterbirth.

4 After birth, a baby lemon shark heads for the safety of the mangroves at the edge of the lagoon. It spends the first few years of its life in a strip of mangrove 120 ft wide and 1,200 ft long, feeding on small fish, worms and shellfish, and being careful to avoid sharks larger than itself. Its home overlaps the territory of other young sharks.

5 To avoid being eaten, young lemon sharks gather with others of the same size. Each group patrols its own section of the lagoon at Bimini. This young lemon shark is about one year old. When it is seven or eight, it will leave the safety of the lagoon and head for the open reefs outside.

# Look in any Ocean

Sharks live throughout the world's oceans and seas, and at all depths. Some sharks, like bull sharks, even swim in rivers and lakes. Whale, reef and nurse sharks are all tropical species that prefer warm waters. Temperate-water sharks, such as the mako, horn and basking sharks, live in water that is 50–68°F. Cold-water sharks often live in very deep water. The Portuguese shark, frilled shark and goblin shark are all cold water sharks. A few species will swim in extremely cold waters, such as the Greenland shark, which braves the icy water around the Arctic Circle.

NORTH
AMERICA

ATLANTIC
OCEAN

PACIFIC
OCEAN

SOUTH
AMERICA

### ▶ SWIMMING POOLS

This map shows the main parts of the world's seas in which different kinds of sharks live. The key beneath the map shows which sharks live where.

### ▶ OCEAN WANDERER

The oceanic whitetip shark swims the world's deep, open oceans, in tropical and subtropical waters. It is also one of the first sharks to appear at shipwrecks.

**KEY**

whale shark

basking shark

bull shark

tiger shark

white tip shark

Greenland shark

great white shark

### ◀ ISLAND LIVING

The Galapagos shark (*Carcharhinus galapagensis*) swims in the waters of the Galapagos islands, on the Equator. It also swims around tropical islands in the Pacific, Atlantic and Indian oceans.

**◄ UNDER THE ICE**
The Greenland shark (*Somniosus microcephalus*) is the only shark known to survive under polar ice in the North Atlantic seas. It has a luminous parasite attached to each eye that attracts prey to the area around its mouth.

**▲ TEMPERATE PREDATOR**
The great white shark lives in temperate, subtropical and tropical seas, including the Mediterranean. It usually swims in coastal waters.

**▲ TIGER OF THE SEAS**
The tiger shark swims in mainly tropical and warm temperate waters, both in open ocean, and close to shore. Tiger sharks have been seen off Morocco and the Canary Islands.

**◄ REEF SHARK**
The blacktip reef shark patrols reefs in the Indian and Pacific oceans. It also lives in the Mediterranean and Red Sea, and as far west as the seas off Tunisia, in North Africa.

103

# Upwardly Mobile

Not all sharks travel far afield. Some prefer to stay close to home, swimming only in one small area. Others have a daily routine, spending the day in deep waters, but moving closer to shore to feed at night. A few deep sea sharks make a different daily journey, spending the day in the deep, and rising to the surface to feed at night. Some sharks travel vast distances, crossing oceans. This has only recently been discovered, with the tagging of sharks. Rather than killing sharks when they catch them, scientists and fishermen now give them a special tag. Each tag has its own number, which identifies the shark. So, when the shark is caught again, scientists can see how much it has grown, and also how far it has traveled.

**sandbar shark**
*(Carcharinus plumbeus)*

**Did you know?** A blue shark once traveled a distance of 966 mi.

**▲ INTO THE GULF**
Atlantic sandbar sharks can travel over 1,875 mi., from the Atlantic coastline to the coast of Mexico. These amazing sharks grow incredibly slowly, only about 1¼ in. a year. They reach adulthood very late in life, when they are 30 years old.

**◄ GIVEN A NAME**
This tiger shark has been tagged (marked) by scientists and is being released back into the sea. Tagging has shown that tiger sharks travel great distances across oceans. Previously people had believed that they stayed in one place.

**◄ OCEAN MIGRATOR**
Female blue sharks in the North Atlantic go on a very long migration. They circle the Atlantic Ocean, mating off North America and then giving birth near Spain and Portugal at the end of their journey.

**► EPIC JOURNEY**
Female blue sharks travel from North America to Europe, where they give birth to their pups. Then they turn back toward the United States. They travel at about 25 mi. per day. A shark swimming fast might cover the round trip of 9,375 mi. in 15 months.

**▼ FOLLOW THE TEMPERATURE**
Shortfin mako sharks travel into the North Atlantic, but rarely swim the whole way across. They like to swim in an exact temperature of 62–71°F. They follow thermal water corridors through the ocean to winter in the Sargasso Sea.

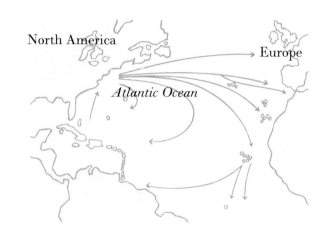

**shortfin mako shark**
*(Isurus oxyrinchus)*

**► DOUBLE BACK**
Migrating mako sharks travel to the middle of the Atlantic Ocean and then turn back toward the United States. The sharks do not go further because from the middle of the ocean to Europe the water is not the temperature they prefer to swim in.

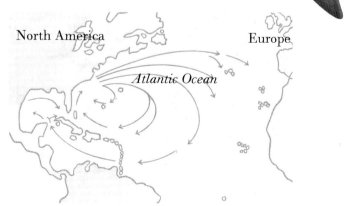

**frilled shark**
*(Chlamydoselachus anguineus)*

# The Ocean Depths

Many sharks are rarely seen because they live in the darkness of the deep. Catsharks and dogfish live in these gloomy waters, glowing in the dark with a luminous green-blue or white light. Some of these species travel and hunt in packs, following their prey to the surface at night, returning into the depths by day. Most of the world's smallest sharks live here. Pygmy and dwarf sharks no bigger than a cigar travel up and down the ocean for several miles each day. On the deep sea floor are such enormous sharks as the sixgill, sevengill and sleeper sharks. These eat the remains of food that sinks down from the sea's surface. Many deep sea sharks look primitive, but strangest of all are the frilled and horned goblin sharks. These look like the fossilized sharks that swam the seas 150 million years ago.

## ▲ LIVING FOSSIL

The frilled shark is the only shark shaped like an eel. It has six feathery gill slits, 300 tiny, three-pointed teeth and a large pair of eyes. Instead of a backbone, it has a firm, but flexible, rod of cartilage. These features tell us that the frilled shark resembles sharks that lived in the oceans millions of years ago.

## ▲ DEEP SEA JOURNEYS

The shortnose spurdog can be recognized by a spine at the front of each dorsal fin. It lives in large packs made up of thousands of sharks. It swims at depths of 2,400 ft in the northern waters of the Atlantic and Pacific oceans. Seasonally, the packs make a daily migration, from north to south and from coastal to deeper waters.

**shortnose spurdog**
*(Squalus megalops)*

## ▼ DEEPEST OF THE DEEP

The Portuguese dogfish holds the record for living in the deepest waters. One was caught 8,154 ft below the sea's surface. At this depth, the water temperature is no higher than a chilly 41–43°F.

**Portuguese dogfish**
*(Centroscymnus coelolepis)*

### ◄ SIXGILL SLITS

Most modern sharks have five gill slits, but primitive sharks, like bluntnose sixgill sharks (*Hexanchus griseus*), have more. These sharks are found at huge depths around the world. They have evolved (developed) slowly, and still have the features of sharks that lived millions of years ago.

### ▼ SEVENGILL SLITS

Broadnose sevengill sharks have seven gill slits. They have primitive, sharp teeth that look like tiny combs. They use these to slice up ratfish, small sharks and mackerel. Because some of their prey live near the surface, sevengill sharks travel to the sea's surface to hunt at night.

**Broadnose sevengill shark**
(*Notorynchus cepedianus*)

**Did you know?** Many deep-sea sharks have light-organs on their bodies.

**velvet belly**
(*Etmopterus spinax*)

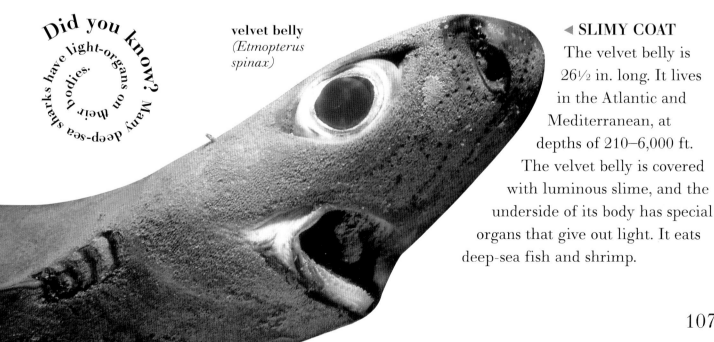

### ◄ SLIMY COAT

The velvet belly is 26½ in. long. It lives in the Atlantic and Mediterranean, at depths of 210–6,000 ft. The velvet belly is covered with luminous slime, and the underside of its body has special organs that give out light. It eats deep-sea fish and shrimp.

# Freshwater Sharks

Although most sharks live in the salt water of the sea, some, such as the bonnethead and sandbar sharks, swim to the mouths of rivers to give birth. There are a few sharks that swim all the way up rivers, and some swim into freshwater lakes. Atlantic sharpnose and spadenose sharks, and Ganges and Borneo river sharks, swim in fresh water. Bull sharks are the species most often seen in fresh water. How this species' body copes with fresh water is not known. A fish that usually swims in salt water needs to find a way of coping with water that is not salt. On entering a river or lake, a fish used to salt water would be expected to absorb water and blow up like a balloon, but bull sharks do not. Somehow, they have found a way to keep the levels of salt in their blood low, thereby reducing water absorption in fresh water.

▲ **HOLY RIVER**
Shark attacks on pilgrims bathing in the holy Ganges River in India were once blamed on the Ganges river shark. Instead, they were probably made by the bull shark, which feeds on cremated bodies thrown into the river.

◄ **RIVER JOURNEYS**
Bull sharks have been seen in the Amazon, Congo and Mississippi rivers, and in other tropical rivers and lakes around the world. They gather at the river mouth, where edible rubbish is found during floods. Bull sharks are also sometimes called Zambezi sharks because they make regular journeys up Africa's Zambezi river.

*Vishnu*
*In Hindu religion, the god Vishnu is believed to be the protector of the world. In legendary tales, Vishnu saved the sacred religious texts of India when the whole world was covered in water. This Indian picture shows him emerging from the mouth of a monstrous fish, probably a shark.*

▲ **KEYS SWIMMER**
This bonnethead shark (*Sphyma tiburo*) lives near river mouths in the Florida Keys.

▶ **BORN-AGAIN SHARK**
The Borneo river shark (*Glyphis*) was believed extinct until one was caught in 1997 by a fisherman in Sabah in Southeast Asia. Until then, the only known specimen was 100 years old and displayed in an Austrian museum.

**Borneo river shark**
*(Glyphis)*

◀ **LAKE NICARAGUA**
Although they do not live all year in Lake Nicaragua in Central America, bull sharks (*Carcharhinus leucas*) are also called Nicaragua sharks because they travel between the lake and the Caribbean Sea. It is thought that some female bull sharks swim to the lake in order to give birth to their pups.

# Life on the Seabed

People once thought that all sharks died unless they kept swimming. This is not true. Many sharks that live close to the sea floor do so without moving for long periods of time. Wobbegong and angel sharks have flattened bodies that help them lie close to the sea floor. Their skin color also blends in with their background, hiding them from their prey as they lie in wait. These sharks take in water through a special spiracle (hole) behind their eye to keep their gills from becoming clogged with sand. Some sharks that live on the sea floor, such as catsharks and carpet sharks, are not flattened. Whatever their shape, most are camouflaged with spots, stripes or a mottled pattern on their back.

▲ **OCEAN CAMOUFLAGE**

Sharks that live near the surface can also camouflage themselves. From above, the great white's dark back blends in with the ocean depths.

▼ **SPOTTED ZEBRA**

The adult zebra shark (*Stegostoma fasciatum*) has spots instead of zebra stripes. It has stripes on its skin as a pup. These break up into spots as the shark grows. It lives in the Indian and Pacific Oceans.

## ▲ CORAL COPYCAT

This tasseled wobbegong (*Eucrossorhinus dasypogon*) is invisible to its prey. It copies colors of rock and coral, and has a fringe of tassels hanging down below its mouth that look like seaweed.

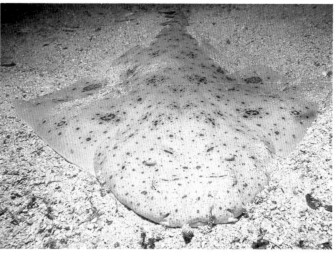

## ▲ AMBUSH EXPERT

The Pacific angel shark (*Squatina californica*) buries itself in the sand, and watches for prey. When a fish comes close, the shark rises up and engulfs the fish in its huge mouth. It then sinks back to the seabed, swallowing its food whole.

## ► SHELLFISH EATER

The leopard shark lives in the shallow waters of the Pacific, along the west coast of the United States. It swims slowly, searching the sea floor for the mollusks that it eats.

## ◄ JAGGED SNOUT

The common sawshark (*Pristiophorus cirratus*) has a long snout with tooth-like barbs along each side. Two sensitive barbels (bristles) hang beneath its snout. It mows through sand and seaweed on the seabed, catching its prey by slashing around with its barbed snout.

111

# Shark Relatives

Sharks have some close relatives. Skates and rays are especially similar to their shark cousins. Both have features that are found in sharks, including a cartilage skeleton, electrical sensors and skin teeth. In fact, skates and rays look like flattened sharks. They also come in all shapes and sizes, ranging from long guitarfish to giant manta rays. Like whale sharks, manta rays also filter plankton from the surface of the sea, but in a more unusual way. Turning somersaults in the water, the rays guide the plankton into their mouths with flattened horns on either side of their head. Another close relative of the shark is the ratfish. Looking like a cross between a shark and a bony fish, the ratfish is probably the long-lost descendant of mollusk-eating sharks that lived 300 million years ago.

## ▲ STING IN THE TAIL

One of 30 known species of sting ray, the southern sting ray (*Dasyatis americana*) moves through the water by rippling its broad pectoral fins. It uses its tail to dish out a barbed sting to any attacker.

## ▼ UNDERSEA RATS

Although they are relatives, ratfish look quite different from sharks. In fact, in some ways they resemble rats. They have a long, thin tail, smooth skin and rodent-like teeth. Male ratfish also have an extra, hooked clasper on their forehead, and use two pairs of claspers around their pelvic fins to grip the females.

**ratfish**
(*Hydrolagus colliei*)

**shovelnose guitarfish**
(*Rhinobatus productus*)

## ▶ SHARK OR RAY?

The long, flat shovelnose guitarfish looks like a cross between a shark and a ray. Although it uses its tail to swim, it is more closely related to rays. It swims in the coastal waters of the eastern Pacific. An adult usually grows to 4½ ft long.

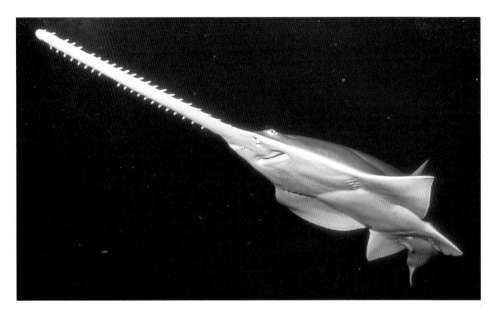

## ◀ SAW FISH

Saw fish (*Pristidae*) belong to the ray family. Unlike sawsharks, the pectoral fins of the saw fish grow forward on its body, and are joined to the side of its head. Its gill openings are found on the underside of its head. It has a broad saw, which is lined with skin teeth that have been especially adapted for hunting.

**electric ray**
(*Torpedo torpedo*)

## ◀ ELECTRIC SHOCK

Torpedo, or electric, rays have special blocks of muscle in their wings that can produce electric shocks of up to 220 volts. They use this hidden weapon to knock out their prey. The shock can stun a human.

**Did you know?** Manta rays may grow to 21 ft across and weigh 3,500 lbs.

## ▶ FLYING RAYS

Spotted eagle rays (*Aetobatus narinaria*) have broad pectoral fins that they flap like birds. The fins of some species span nearly 12 ft. Spotted eagle rays feed on shellfish and oysters, which they crush with their teeth.

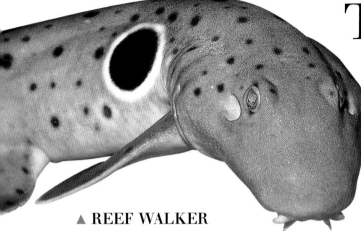

# The Eight Families

Sharks fall into eight main orders (groups) divided according to different features. The most primitive orders, including frilled and sevengill sharks, have more than five gill slits. Dogfish sharks have long, round bodies, and include luminous (glow in the dark) sharks that live in very deep water. The seven or more species of sawshark have a saw-like snout. Angel sharks look like rays and lie hidden on the seabed. Bullhead sharks have spines on both of their dorsal fins, and carpet sharks, like the wobbegong sharks, have short snouts and bristles on their snouts. Mackerel sharks, with their special, warm muscles, are awesome hunters. These sharks include the great white and mako. The ground sharks include the widest range of all, from catsharks to bull sharks, hammerheads, blue sharks and oceanic whitetips.

▲ **REEF WALKER**
Two pairs of muscular pectoral fins allow the epaulette shark (*Hemiscyllium ocellatum*) to walk over its tropical reef home. It feeds on the seabeds of shallow waters around the Australian reefs.

▼ **TYPES OF SHARKS**
Modern sharks are divided into eight large family groups. These groups are divided into over 30 smaller families, and nearly 400 species. This number will probably rise, as more species of shark are discovered.

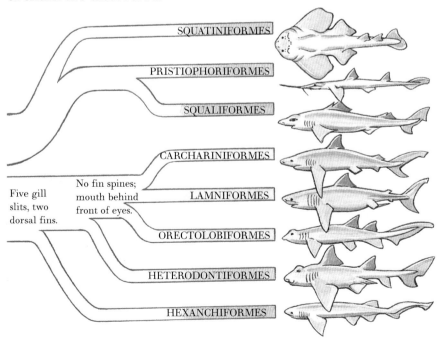

|  |  |
|---|---|
| SQUATINIFORMES | Body flattened, raylike. Mouth in front. |
| PRISTIOPHORIFORMES | Snout elongated and sawlike. Mouth underneath. |
| SQUALIFORMES | Snout short, not sawlike. |
| CARCHARINIFORMES | Sliding flap that covers eyes. |
| LAMNIFORMES | No sliding flap over eyes. |
| ORECTOLOBIFORMES | Mouth well in front of eyes. |
| HETERODONTIFORMES | Dorsal fin spines. |
| HEXANCHIFORMES | Six or seven gill slits. One dorsal fin. |

No fin spines; mouth behind front of eyes.

Five gill slits, two dorsal fins.

## ◄ PRIMITIVE SHARK

The broadnose sevengill shark (*Notorynchus cepedianus*) is one of five species of primitive shark. Each has six or seven gill slits. All swim in deep waters.

## ▲ GROUND SHARK

The swell shark (*Cephaloscyllium ventriosum*) is a ground shark. It blows up like a balloon by swallowing water and storing it in its stomach. When it is threatened, this amazing shark wedges itself firmly inside the cracks between rocks. It can be very difficult to remove.

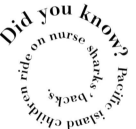

Did you know? Pacific Island children ride on nurse sharks' backs.

*Food for the sharks*
*The Carib peoples buried the bodies of their dead relatives by ceremonially putting them into Lake Nicaragua in Central America. Many of the bodies were then eaten by bull sharks in the lake. One thief made a fortune by catching the sharks, slitting them open and removing jewels that had decorated the bodies of the dead. Until he was caught, that is . . .*

## ► REQUIEM SHARK

The sandbar, or brown, shark (*Carcharhinus plumbeus*) is a requiem shark—here, requiem means "ceremony for the dead." All members of this family are active hunters. They rule tropical seas, hunting fish, squid and sea turtles. They are probably the most modern group of shark.

# Friends and Enemies

No sharks spend all their time alone. They attract all kinds of hangers-on, including pilot fish, bait fish and a wide range of parasites, both inside their bodies and out! Sandtiger sharks are often seen surrounded by a cloud of baby bait fish. Too small for the shark to eat, the bait fish crowd around it for protection. Basking sharks are sometimes covered with sea lampreys, which clamp on to the shark's skin with their sucker-like mouths. To get rid of these pests, the giant sharks leap out of the water and crash back down to dislodge them. Smaller parasites live inside each shark. These have adapted so well to life with sharks that they can only survive in one species, some in only one part of the shark's digestive system.

## ▲ STRIPED PILOTS

Tiny pilot fish often ride the bow wave in front of a shark's snout. Young golden trevally fish swim with whale sharks. When they are older and lose their stripes, they leave the shark and return to their reef homes.

## ▼ HITCHHIKER

A remora fish stays with a shark for most of its life. Its dorsal fin is designed like a sucker, which the fish uses to attach itself to the shark's belly. The fish then feeds on scraps from the shark's meal.

► **SCRAPING CURE**

Some fish use the shark's rough, sandpaper-like skin to remove their own parasites. Rainbow runner fish will rub against a whitetip reef shark's side. Behind one shark might be an entire group of fish lining up for a scrub.

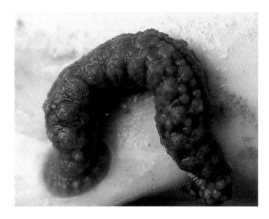

◄ **BARBER SHOP**

Many sharks visit what scientists call cleaning stations. Here, small fish and shrimps remove dead skin and parasites from the shark's body, even entering the gills and mouth. This hammerhead shark is gliding past a cleaning station where several king angel fish have darted out to clean it.

▼ **UNWELCOME FRIENDS**

Strings of parasitic copepod eggs trail behind the dorsal fin of this shortfin mako shark. These parasites will have little effect on the shark's life, but if large numbers of parasites grow inside the shark, it can die.

► **BLOOD SUCKER**

A marine leech feeds by attaching itself to any part of the shark's skin and sucking its blood. Other parasites feed only on certain areas of the shark's body, like the gills, mouth and nasal openings.

*Did you know? Pilot fish ride sharks' bow waves like dolphins on ships.*

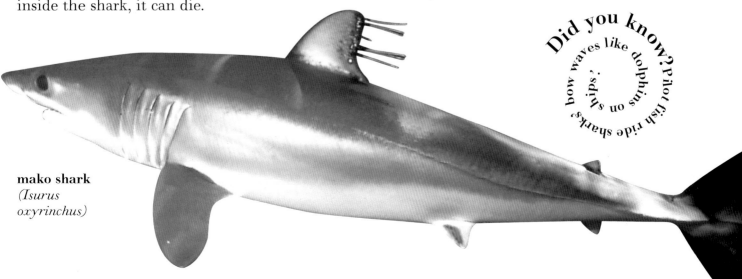

**mako shark**
*(Isurus oxyrinchus)*

# Sharks and People

Sharks are feared because they attack people. However, only a few such attacks take place each year. People are more likely to be killed on the way to the beach than killed by a shark in the water. Fortunately, attitudes are changing. Today, people have a healthy respect for sharks, rather than a fear of them. As we come to understand sharks, instead of killing them, we want to learn more about them. Diving with sharks, even such known threats as the great white shark or bull shark, is more accepted. People study sharks either from the safety of a cage or, increasingly, in the open sea without any protection. Such is our fascination with sharks that aquariums are being built all over the world. Here, more people will be able to learn about sharks first hand, and not even get wet!

### Jaws
*The book and film* Jaws *featured an enormous great white shark that terrorized a seaside town. The film drew great crowds, and its story terrified people all over the world. It also harmed the reputation of sharks, encouraging people to see them as monsters, rather than the extraordinarily fascinating animals that they are.*

### ◀ FEEDING TIME
At tourist resorts in the tropics, divers can watch sharks being fed by hand. This activity is not always approved of. Sharks come to rely on these free handouts, and may become aggressive if it stops. Inexperienced divers may also not know how to behave with sharks, resulting in accidents, although these are rare.

### ◄ ANTI-SHARK MEASURES

Anti-shark nets protect many popular South African and Australian beaches. Unfortunately, these nets not only catch sharks, like this tiger shark, but also other sea life, including dolphins and turtles. Less destructive ways of reducing people's fear of attack have yet to be invented.

### ► SHARK POD

Although a similar system is not yet available to bathers, one anti-shark invention seems to work for divers and, possibly, surfers, too. A shark pod can produce an electric field that interferes with the electrical sensors of a shark, encouraging the animal to keep its distance.

### ◄ SHARK ATTACK

Occasionally, sharks do attack. While diving in Australian waters, Rodney Fox was attacked by a great white shark. Rodney was possibly mistaken for a seal. He is probably alive because he did not have enough blubber on him to interest the shark and he was able to get away.

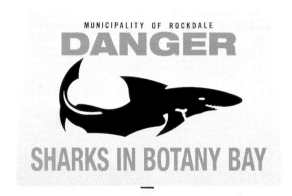

MUNICIPALITY OF ROCKDALE
## DANGER
## SHARKS IN BOTANY BAY

### ▲ SHARK WARNING

On many beaches, shark warning signs are used to tell people that sharks might be present. During the day, danger of attack is low, but it increases at night, when the sharks move inshore to feed.

119

# *Focus on the Great*

The great white shark grows to over 18 feet long and is the largest hunting fish in the sea. Its powerful jaws can bite a full-grown elephant seal in half. Many people believe that the great white will attack people readily. This is not true. In the whole world, only about ten people a year are bitten by great whites. Great whites are aggressive, powerful fish and will attack people when they mistake them for their natural prey, such as seals. If they realize their mistake, there is a chance that a person can survive—that is, if the blood loss from the first bite can be stopped.

### INTELLIGENT SHARK
The great white shows signs of 'intelligent' planning. It stakes out places off the Farallon Islands to the west of San Francisco, CA, where young elephant seals swim. In this way it avoids the large, possibly aggressive, adult bulls that could do it damage.

### BODY PERFECT
The great white has the torpedo shape typical of a hunting shark. Its crescent-shaped tail, with its equal upper and lower parts, helps the shark to speed through the water. Although it is called the great white, it is not white all over, but gray on top and white underneath.

120

# *White Shark*

## GIANT SHARK ENCOUNTER

A great white shark dwarfs any diver. To a diver in a cage, it can sometimes seem that a shark is trying to attack. In reality, the shark's electrical sensors are probably confused. The diver's metal cage produces an electrical field in seawater—the shark is then likely to react to the cage as if it were prey.

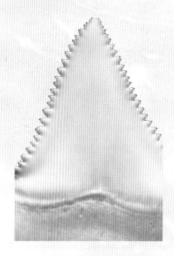

## TERRIBLE JAWS

As a great white rises to take bait, its black eyes roll back into their protective sockets. Its jaws thrust forward, filled with rows of triangular teeth ready to take a bite. This incredible action takes place in little more than a second.

## SHARP TEETH

The powerful, arrow-shaped teeth in the upper jaw of a great white have a serrated (jagged) edge. These teeth can slice through flesh, blubber and even bone. The shark saws through the tissue of its prey by shaking its head from side to side.

## GAME FISH

To fishermen who hunt great whites for sport, the large breeding female sharks are the most attractive. The killing of these sharks has brought them near extinction in some places.

# Conservation

Sharks take a long time to grow to adulthood. They have very few offspring and may breed only every other year. Added to these factors, the hunting and killing of sharks can quickly reduce their numbers. This happened at Achill Island, on the Irish coast, where large numbers of basking sharks quickly disappeared, killed for their oil. Off the coasts of South Australia and South Africa, the great white shark was hunted as a trophy for many years. Numbers of great whites were so reduced that the hunting of them has since been banned internationally. A few countries control the fishing of sharks, to try to conserve (protect) them. However, in other countries, sharks are still hunted to be used in shark fin soup, unusual medicines and souvenirs. They are also sold to supermarkets as shark steak. Sharks, it seems, have more to fear from people than people have to fear from sharks.

**◄ WASTED SHARKS**
Each summer, sharks are killed in fishing tournaments off the east coast of the United States. Sports fisherman are now learning to tag sharks, returning them to the sea alive instead of killing them. By tagging sharks, our understanding of shark biology is increased.

► **CRUEL TRADE**
Caught by fishermen, this whitetip reef shark has had its valuable fins removed. The shark was then thrown back into the sea, still alive. Without its fins, a shark is unable to move and, therefore, feed. It will quickly starve to death. This awful process, called finning, has been banned by some countries.

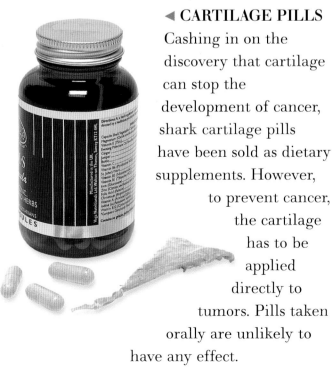

◄ **TRAVELING INTO TROUBLE**
This tiger shark is being tagged to track its movements. Shark-tagging programs like this show that many sharks traveling great distances are being netted by several fisheries along their routes. Unless shark fishing is controlled internationally, far-traveling sharks will probably disappear from the sea altogether.

◄ **CARTILAGE PILLS**
Cashing in on the discovery that cartilage can stop the development of cancer, shark cartilage pills have been sold as dietary supplements. However, to prevent cancer, the cartilage has to be applied directly to tumors. Pills taken orally are unlikely to have any effect.

▲ **MULTIMILLION DOLLAR SOUP**
Shark fin soup is made from the dried fins of sharks. It has been prepared by chefs in Asian countries for over 2,000 years. The soup was once served to show favor to an honored guest, and was also thought to be a health-giving food. Today, it is sold in cans and can be bought at supermarkets.

# GLOSSARY

**afterbirth**
Any birth membranes and other tissues discarded or discharged into the sea when a baby shark is born.

**Antarctic**
The region around the South Pole and Southern Ocean, including the continent of Antarctica.

**Arctic**
The region around the North Pole.

**baleen**
A tough and flexible material, which forms comb-like plates in the upper jaw of baleen whales.

**baleen whale**
A whale that has baleen plates in its mouth instead of teeth.

**beak**
The protruding jaws of a whale or dolphin.

**bioluminescence**
The production of light by living organisms.

**blow**
The cloud of moist air that is blown from a whale's blowhole when it breathes out.

**blowhole**
The nostril of a whale. Baleen whales have two blowholes, toothed whales have one.

**blubber**
The layer of fatty tissue beneath the skin of a whale that acts as insulation against cold water.

**bow-riding**
Swimming on the bow wave in front of a moving boat.

**breaching**
Leaping out of the water and falling back with a great splash.

**bull**
A male whale.

**calf**
A baby whale.

**cartilage**
The strong but flexible material from which the skeletons of sharks and rays are made, rather than the bone that is found in most other animals with backbones.

**catshark**
The common name given to a group of sharks that are known in the British Isles as dogfish.

**cetacean**
A whale, dolphin or porpoise, all of which belong to the animal order Cetacea.

**clasper**
The male sexual organs in sharks, consisting of two modified pelvic fins.

**cow**
A female whale.

**crustacean**
A creature with a hard body that lives in the sea. Shrimp and krill are crustaceans.

**dolphin**
A small, toothed whale that has cone-shaped teeth.

**dorsal fin**
The usually triangular fin on the back of a whale's body and the tall triangular fin on a shark's back. Some sharks have two dorsal fins, the front fin larger than the back one.

**echo-location**
The method toothed whales use to find their prey. They send out pulses of high-pitched sounds and listen for the echoes produced when the pulses are reflected by objects in their path.

**egg case**
The leathery covering that protects a shark embryo developing outside its mother's body.

**electrical field**
A zone of electricity surrounding an object, such as a muscle or nerve cell, that generates electricity.

**feeding frenzy**
The name for what happens when sharks go berserk, slashing and biting anything that moves, when there is blood in the water or when they are presented with large quantities of food.

**filter-feeder**
Animals that sieve water through giant combs called gill rakers, for very small particles of food.

**fish ball**
The ball that schools of fish make when attacked.

**flipper**
A whale's paddle-like forelimbs.

**flukes**
The tail of a whale.

**fluking**
Raising the flukes into the air before diving.

**gestation**
The period of time between conception and the birth of an animal.

**gill arch**
The part of the skeleton that supports the gills.

**gill slit**
The vertical openings on either side of the shark, just behind the head, from which the water taken in through the mouth and passed over the gills leaves its body.

**gills**
The organ used by aquatic animals, such as sharks, for breathing.

**gut**
The long tube in which food is digested and absorbed, running a winding path through an animal's body.

**jawless fish**
Primitive fish with sucker-like mouths rather than true jaws. Their origins were 500 million years ago, and living descendants include lampreys and hagfish.

**krill**
Small shrimp-like creatures that swim in huge shoals. Krill form part of the diet of filter feeders such as whale sharks. They are also the main food for many of the baleen whales.

**light organs**
Special structures in a fish's skin that produce 'cold' light. They work either by mixing particular chemicals together or with the help of luminous bacteria that do it for them.

**lob-tailing**
Raising the tail into the air and then slapping it down on the surface of the water.

**mammal**
An animal that has warm blood and breathes air. Female mammals feed their offspring on milk from their mammary glands.

**mating**
When a male and female unite to reproduce.

**megalodon**
A gigantic shark ancestor that first appeared 18 million years ago. It is thought to be the ancestor of the great white shark.

**melon**
The rounded forehead of a toothed whale. It is thought to help direct the sounds the animal uses for echo-location.

**migration**
The regular journey taken by some animals from one region to another and back at different times of the year.

**nutrients**
Chemicals in food that, when digested, build blood, bone and tissue. This tissue maintains growth and strength in the body.

**parasite**
An organism that lives on or in another living thing (its host), using the host as a source of food and shelter.

**pectoral fin**
An alternative name for flipper.

**pectoral fins**
The pair of large wing-like fins on either side of a shark's body.

**pelvic fins**
The pair of small fins on the underside of a shark's body behind the pectoral fins.

**placenta**
A disk-shaped organ that is attached to the lining of the womb during pregnancy. It is through this that the embryo receives oxygen and nutrients.

**plankton**
Tiny sea creatures and plants that drift with the water movements in the sea or in lakes. They form the basic foodstuff for all life in the oceans.

**pod**
A group of whales.

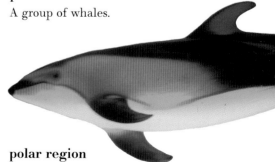

**polar region**
The area around the North or South Pole, where it is very cold.

**porpoise**
A small-toothed whale with spade-shaped teeth.

**porpoising**
Leaping in and out of the water while swimming fast.

**predator**
An animal that hunts other animals (prey) for its food.

**pregnant**
When a female animal has a baby developing in her womb.

**prey**
Animals that are hunted for food by others (predators).

**primitive**
Keeping physical characteristics that may have origins millions of years ago.

**pup**
A young shark, particularly when it has just been born.

**pupil**
The opening, which can be round or slit-like, through which light passes to the eye of an animal.

**receptor**
A cell or part of a cell that is designed to respond to a particular stimulus such as light, heat or smell.

**remora**
A streamlined fish that attaches itself to a shark's body with a sucker, and accompanies its larger companion everywhere.

**rorqual**
A baleen whale with grooves in its throat. The grooves allow the throat to expand when the animal is taking in water when it is feeding

**scavenger**
An animal that feeds on animals that have died naturally or were the prey of other predators.

**school**
Another name for a group of whales.

**sensory system**
The collection of cells and organs through which an animal is able to receive messages from its surroundings.

**species**
A group of individuals that can breed successfully together. When naming animals scientifically, this is the basic unit of classification.

**spiracle**
A modified gill slit positioned behind the eye in sharks and rays.

**spiral valve**
A complicated folding of the tissues in the intestine of sharks that aids efficient digestion of nutrients.

**splashguard**
A raised area in front of the blowholes of some whales. It helps prevent water entering the blowholes when the whales breathe.

**spout**
Spout is another word for blow.

**spy-hopping**
Poking the head out of the water so that the eyes are above the surface.

**stranding**
Coming out of the water on to the shore and becoming stuck, or stranded.

**streamlined**
Shaped to slip through the water easily without much resistance.

**tail fin**
Another name for a whale's flukes.

**temperate**
A climate in which the weather is not too hot and not too cold.

**thermal corridor**
A layer of water at a particular temperature.

**threat display**
The aggressive behavior shown by some species of shark when confronted by other sharks or sea creatures.

**tooth whorl**
A spiral arrangement of the teeth in some species of extinct sharks.

**toothed whale**
A whale that has teeth and not baleen plates in its mouth. Toothed whales include sperm whales, dolphins and porpoises.

**tropical**
The climate in the Tropics, the region on either side of the Equator, where the seas are always warm.

**vertical migration**
The daily movement that sharks make downward into the deep sea by day and upward to the surface waters at night.

**whale**
A cetacean. Commonly the term is applied to the large whales, such as the baleen and sperm whales.

**whalebone**
A popular name for baleen, but baleen is not bone.

**whaling**
Hunting whales for their meat and blubber.

**yolk sac**
An outgrowth of the embryo's gut containing food that sustains the shark embryo before it is born. As the yolk is used up the sac is withdrawn into the embryo's body.

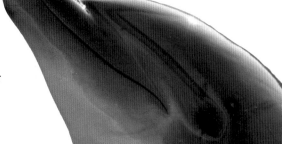

# INDEX

## PICTURE CREDITS